Nuggets of Truth For 365 Days

Sara Haywood

Nuggets of Truth For 365 Days

Copyright © 2016 by Sara Haywood

Published by:
Theocentric Publishing Group
1069A Main Street
Chipley, Florida 32428

www.theocentricpublishing.com
All rights reserved. No part of this book may be reproduced or transmitted in any form or by any means without written permission of the author.

Scripture taken from the Amplified Bible, Copyright © 1954, 1958, 1962, 1964, 1965, 1987 by The Lockman Foundation. Used by permission.

Scripture taken from the New King James Version®. Copyright © 1982 by Thomas Nelson. Used by permission. All rights reserved.

Library of Congress Control Number: 2017945952

ISBN 9780998560618

This Book is dedicated to Father God, who is the "Lover of my soul," and because of Him all blessings flows. Still, being prompted and revealed through the Holy Spirit, known as the "Spirit of Truth," who birth this vision during my prayer and worship times. I am humbled by this awesome experience and challenge you to pursue your visions and dreams in Jesus name!

Yet my loving husband, Willie his voice Conveyed: "You must spend some time on this project every day because "Faith without works is dead." Thank you for encouraging me on a daily basis to move forward by faith. Still, my beautiful children: Lamonzo, Shanell, Naomi, thank you for being by my side over the years. I love you unconditionally!

While, these God fearing warriors reminded me to press on and be obedient to this God given assignment there are blessings in obedience. The Lord is taking me to another level in Him. Special thanks to the following friends: "Annie Daniels, Arrie Mae Daniels, Charmane Jones Gaskin, Cora Helms, Maevine Morris, Macie Salter and Theresa Sherman."

"Therefore we also pray always for you that our God would count you worthy of this calling, and fulfill all the good pleasure of His goodness and the work of faith with power."
2 Thessalonians 1:11

Preface

Nuggets of truth was written as a tool designed to complement as a comprehensive, personal and intimate study of the word of God. "In the beginning was the Word, and the Word was with God, and the Word was God. He was in the beginning with God" (John 1:1-2). The Bible is the foundation of all spiritual truths that will compel one to dig deeper in God's word. The promises of the Lord are concealed in the Bible for one to search it out like hunting for treasure. "It is the glory of God to conceal a matter, but the glory of kings is to search out a matter" (Proverbs 25:2).

Man always feels the need to find out; God never does because He already knows! After all, he who hungers and thirst after righteousness shall be filled. If you are hungry or thirsty He will feed you and satisfy your thirsty souls. Get ready to receive a continual feast! Before you begin your journey of studying the word of the Lord make prayer your first priority. Prayer is monologue and dialogue. For, this reason, "Men shall always pray and not faint" (Luke 18:1).

After praying invite the Holy Spirit to be your guide while yielding to His "still small voice", being thoroughly persuaded and fully convinced by relying on His work in you. As He transforms one no other human can take credit for this. God gets all the glory.

Although, the word of the Lord can be compared to Nuggets of truth, the word of God is a seed (Luke 8:11). You will discover many living seeds in this instrument that will shape your life into God's divine plans and direction for you and your family. That is if one adheres and mixes the word with faith.

Now, the Bible is the exploratory field for godly living, biblical truths resulting as the final authority, roadmap, daily guide and heavenly destination. We are instructed in the word of the Lord as follows:

> I beseech you therefore brethren by the mercies of God, that you present your bodies a living sacrifice, holy, acceptable to God, which is your reasonable service. And do not be conformed to this world, but be transformed by the renewing of your mind, that you may prove that which is good and acceptable and perfect will of God. (Romans 12:1-2)

Even though, one has a God given responsibility to live on the earth as children of light, this transformation starts after a person receives Jesus Christ as Savior. He reminds us in the scripture, "You are the light of the world. A city that is set on a hill cannot be hidden" (Matthew 5:14).

The mercies of the Lord brings benefits to us as Christians, let us respond appropriately by living A Holy, faith filed life before God and man. He is watching and waiting to respond to His Nuggets of truth in the Bible. Will you get involved with the Holy Spirit prompting as one studies, meditated and apply these truths? If you answered yes to this question brace yourself for a new awakening while revelation knowledge and truth invades your inner man – body, soul and spirit! Old things have passed away, behold the new has arrived! Rejoice in Him! Thank you Jesus for your Anointing being released for your project: Nuggets of Truth! After salvation, Christians should represent themselves as God's new creation in Christ Jesus. One should offer our bodies as a living sacrifice on a daily basis by denouncing:

Sin, pride, arrogance, unwholesome speech, self-centeredness, conceit, envy, strife, jealousy, and an unexaggerated opinion of one's self. Remember, it is God who has made us and not ourselves, He is the manufacture, creator of the universe. We are fearfully and wonderfully made; because of His love we are a designer's original. Praise the name of Jesus;

promotion comes from Him! Our task is a simple one: Lift Him up at all times without any shame! If a person is not very careful one may fall into the category of idolatry. This is a dangerous doctrine for anyone to adopt or partake of. The Lord declares: He is a jealous God and will not have any other Gods before Him. When this is prevalent, destruction is lurking in the Shadows awaiting the opportune time to overtake an individual, resulting in death! Only when, one continues to seek passionately after the word of the Lord; our lives will become richer, moisture is being released from the anointing of the "Holy Spirit", like fresh dew on the grass in the morning. A person lifestyle will have more productivity as divine skillful and Godly wisdom is evident for all to behold. When this happens a generation of repentance, spiritual, Holy, dedicated, moral, justified men and women will emerge by being complete in Christ Jesus. He does not show any partiality toward His children. All can learn from this grace. "A wise man will hear and increase in learning, and a man of understanding will attain wise council" (Proverbs 1:5).

After completing this tool Nuggets of truth one will discover un-revealed truths found in God's word! A word spoken in due season, how good it is. Besides, while the earth remains seed time and harvest, winter, summer heat and cold shall never cease. They are waiting to be discovered and applied in our lives. From faith to faith the just shall live by our uncompromisingly faith.

An example of such a truth to ponder and meditate on is, "Call to me, and I will answer you, and show you great and mighty things, which you do not know" (Jeremiah 33:3). In order to receive the maximum benefits of Nuggets of truth one should have a special place of consecration to commune with the Lord on a daily basis. Leave the cell phones, I-pods, tablets, lab tops, any electronic devices off limits. Also, snacks and drinks.

Furthermore, as one engages in prayer this is spiritual warfare. For we do not wrestle against flesh and blood, but against principalities, against powers, against the rulers of the darkness of this age, against spiritual hosts of wickedness in the heavenly places. What will be permitted are clean hands, repentance on our lips, a pure heart, humility, total surrender, transparency of one's soul, yearning to be in the presence of the Lord While worshipping at His feet; being thankful to Him as one bless His Holy and righteous name. Hallelujah to the Lamb of God, He is Sovereign, Majestic, Holy, Holy, Holy is the Lord the earth is filled with His glory. Even though, this is a good time to wave your hands, with palms turned upward in a receiving posture; nothing else matters in this time of worship give to the Lord a wave offering! Oh Bless His name!

> Lift up your heads, O you gates! And be lifted up you everlasting doors! And the King of glory shall come in. Who is this King of glory? The Lord strong and mighty, the Lord mighty in battle. Who is this King of glory? The Lord of host, He is the King of glory. Selah. (Psalm 24: 7-8, 10)

As soon as a person realizes that nothing is hidden in God's presence these victories are manifested: He loose the bonds of wickedness, undo heavy burdens, releases the oppress, binds up the wounded broken and contrite spirit, brings comfort to all who mourns, gives beauty for ashes, the oil of joy for mourning, the garment of praise for the spirit of heaviness that we may be call trees of righteousness the planting of the Lord that He may be glorified.

Now, Abba Father will give us refreshed, renewed, anointing to enable us to remain steadfast, unmovable always abounding in the work of the lord knowing that our labor for Him is not in vain. There is plenty of work to go around no need to shove or push! "Surely the Lord God does nothing, unless He reveals His secret to His servants the prophets" (Amos 3:7).

Can you be trusted with God's word and if so will you share this gospel with others? Selah. God's word is a lamp to our feet and a light to our paths. Watch out and do not allow your steps to be hindered because walking in the darkness is not an option any longer. For the Lord is good His mercy is everlasting and His truths endures to all generations.

    Nuggets of truth is God's project for His people get ready for His word to exhort, edify, comfort and disciple –realize that I'm not exempt from this tool. Everything begins with the word. Remember, it is God who has made us and not ourselves. Commit your way to the LORD, trust also in Him, and He shall give you the desires of your heart. " It is written: Man shall not live by bread alone, but by every word that proceeds from the mouth of God" (Matthew 4:4). Get ready to embark on a new chapter in your relationship with the Lord. If the Lord be lifted up from the earth, He will draw all men to Himself. Finally, after your transformation, while studying, meditating and applying Nuggets of truths; "But you shall receive power when the Holy Spirit has come upon you; and you shall be witnesses to Me in Jerusalem and in all Judea and Samaria and to the end of the earth" (Acts 1:8)

    In Covenant with Him,
    Sara Haywood

Day 1

NUGGETS OF TRUTH

I will bless the Lord at all times; His praise shall continually, be in my mouth.

PSALM 34:1 – AMP.

When we awake in the mornings it
Is vital that we acknowledge Him with
Adorations from our lips.

Comments and Notes:

Day 2

NUGGETS OF TRUTH

The Lord is my Shepherd;
I shall not want.

PSALM 23:1

The more we trust and have confidence
In our creator God, without wavering
In our belief; we shall not lack for anything.
Be advised that this calls for us being a good
Steward over our finances.

Comments and Notes:

_____

_____

_____

_____

_____

_____

Day 3

NUGGETS OF TRUTH

*Lean on, trust in and be confident
In the Lord, with all your
heart and mind
And do not rely on your own
understanding.*

PROVERBS 3:5 - AMP

It is vital that we be fully persuaded;
That the Lord is capable of leading
And guiding us with our best interest
In mind. Also, we must not allow
Our intellect to govern our decisions.

Comments and Notes:

Day 4

NUGGETS OF TRUTH

In all your ways know, recognize, and acknowledge Him, and He will direct and make straight and plain your paths.

PROVERBS 3:6 - AMP

Although we may think that our education
Maybe superior in our decision making,
Godly and supreme wisdom
Supersedes earthly knowledge.

Comments and Notes:

_____

_____

_____

Day 5

NUGGETS OF TRUTH

*For whom the Lord loves
He corrects,
Even as a father corrects the son
In whom he delights.*

PROVERBS 3:12

Just as a parent loves a child
by corrective discipline
Our Heavenly Father chastises us out of love.

Comments and Notes:

_____

_____

_____

_____

_____

Day 6

NUGGETS OF TRUTH

Happy (blessed, fortunate, enviable) is the man who finds skillful and godly Wisdom, And the man who gets understanding, (drawing it Forth from God's Word and life experiences)

PROVERBS 3:13

By realizing the character of Godly wisdom; One will be endowed with heavenly Giftings; that enables us to make spiritual withdrawals for everyday living.

Comments and Notes:

_____

_____

Day 7

NUGGETS OF TRUTH

For the gaining of it is better than the gaining Of silver, and the profit of it is better Than fine gold.

PROVERBS 3:14

The more we chase after Godly supreme wisdom; It far surpasses any type of refined minerals; Precious jewels even the value of gold can't compare To its net worth.

Comments and Notes:

_____

_____

_____

_____

_____

Day 8

NUGGETS OF TRUTH

But for me and my house, We will serve the Lord.

JOSHUA 24:15B

As Parents or leaders of our homes
One must be firm in the faith
Not asking the child if he or she
Wants to attend church
But instructing them they will go with you
Don't just send them;
this is not up for discussion or debate!

Comments and Notes:

_____

_____

_____

_____

Day 9

NUGGETS OF TRUTH

"He sent his word and healed them, And delivered them from their destructions."

PSALM 107:20

One sure way to receive your healing is too Declare and decree, pray the word of God Over your body or circumstances.

Comments and Notes:

_____

_____

_____

_____

Day 10

NUGGETS OF TRUTH

Through the LORD'S mercies we are Not consumed, Because His compassions fail not.

LAMENTATIONS 3:22

The Lord is showing His loving kindness;
To us on a daily basis; still allowing
Us to repent and turn from sin.

Comments and Notes:

_____

_____

_____

_____

_____

Day 11

NUGGETS OF TRUTH

They are new every morning; Great is Your faithfulness.

LAMENTATIONS 3:23

God's grace is extending toward us another Opportunity day by day as We inhale and exhale!!!

Comments and Notes:

_____

_____

_____

_____

_____

_____

Day 12

NUGGETS OF TRUTH

"The LORD is my portion," says my soul," therefore I hope in Him!"

LAMENTATIONS 3:24

"Abba Father is a daily serving"
To our inner man; strengthening
Us from the inside out.

Comments and Notes:

Day 13

NUGGETS OF TRUTH

The LORD is good to those who wait for Him, To the soul who seeks Him.

LAMENTATIONS 3:25

God is a gift;
That we must patiently wait;
To see Him in all His splendor
As we pursue His Love!!!

Comments and Notes:

Day 14

NUGGETS OF TRUTH

Behold, I will do a new thing,
Now it shall spring forth;
Shall you not know it?
I will even make a road
In the wilderness
And rivers in the desert.

ISAIAH 43:19

Watch for the newly acquired gifts;
That are emerging now;
Created highways; with endless waves
Surrounding it from the oceans!!

Comments and Notes:

_____

_____

_____

Day 15

NUGGETS OF TRUTH

*Do not remember the former things,
Nor consider the things of old.*

ISAIAH 43:18

Release past issues and disappointments;
They only hinder your growth and progress
To move forward by Faith!!!

Comments and Notes:

_____

_____

_____

_____

_____

_____

Day 16

NUGGETS OF TRUTH

Put Me in remembrance;
Let us contend together;
State you case, that you may
Be acquitted.

Isaiah 43:26

One must remind the Lord
Concerning our holy lifestyle;
Obedience, and dedication to Him;
By doing so we will be victorious!

Comments and Notes:

_____

_____

_____

_____

_____

Day 17

NUGGETS OF TRUTH

For I will pour water on him who is Thirsty, and floods on the dry ground;
I will pour My Spirit on Your descendants and my blessing On your off-spring.

ISAIAH 44:3

The Lord shall release His anointing
On those who are thirsty for Him;
From one generation to another
All will receive the Abrahamic covenant.

Comments and Notes:

_____

_____

_____

Day 18

NUGGETS OF TRUTH

A good man leaves as inheritance
To his children's children,
But the wealth of the sinner
Is stored up for the righteous.

PROVERBS 13:22

When the righteous are in authority
Our children shall have an inheritance.
The unsaved will make deposits
In our bank accounts!!!

Comments and Notes:

_____

_____

_____

_____

_____

Day 19

NUGGETS OF TRUTH

The simple believes every word,
But the prudent considers well
His steps.

PROVERBS 14:15

Without Godly wisdom one may
Be gullible in our dealings;
The word is a lamp to our feet!

Comments and Notes:

_____

_____

_____

_____

_____

Day 20

NUGGETS OF TRUTH

*The LORD is my strength;
He will make my feet like deer's feet,
And He will make me walk on
High hills.*

HABAKKUK 3:19

As one consults the Lord;
His joy gives us strength, so that
We will be able to adjust with promotion.

Comments and Notes:

_____

_____

_____

_____

_____

Day 21

NUGGETS OF TRUTH

*For all the promises
of God in Him are
Yes, and in Him Amen, to the glory
Of God through us.*

2 CORINTHIANS 2:20

The word of the Lord is guaranteed;
Bringing Him glory as we increase in
The wisdom and knowledge of Him.

Comments and Notes:

_____

_____

_____

_____

_____

Day 22

NUGGETS OF TRUTH

The king's favor is toward
A wise servant,
But his wrath is against him
Who causes shame.

PROVERBS 14:35

A wise son should receive access
Before going in designated areas.
Without permission it's embarrassing.

Comments and Notes:

_____

_____

_____

_____

_____

Day 23

Nuggets of Truth

A soft answer turns away wrath,
But a harsh word stirs up anger.

Proverbs 15:1

A wise person avoids raising
His voice during an argument;
Some things unsaid speaks volumes.

Comments and Notes:

_____

_____

_____

_____

_____

_____

_____

Day 24

NUGGETS OF TRUTH

For we are not as so many,
Peddling the word of God;
But as of sincerity,
But as from God, we speak in
The sight of God in Christ.

2 CORINTHIANS 2:17

Ministers or servants must not
Be for hire; one should minister
Unto the lord for this is
Why we preach Jesus Christ;
Death, burial and resurrection.

Comments and Notes:

_____

_____

_____

Day 25

NUGGETS OF TRUTH

You are our epistles of Christ,
Ministered by us,
Written not with ink,
But by the Spirit of the living God,
Not on tablets of stone
But on tablets of flesh,
That is of the heart.

2 CORINTHIANS 3:3

One must be mindful of our
Conduct; walking upright
Before God and man.

Comments and Notes:

_____

_____

Day 26

NUGGETS OF TRUTH

For in it the righteous of God Is revealed from Faith to Faith; As it is written, the just shall Live by faith.

ROMANS 1:17

When we are born-again
We are justified and declared righteous.
It is here when we simply learn to trust,
And obey without tossing to and fro.

Comments and Notes:

_____

_____

_____

_____

_____

Day 27

NUGGETS OF TRUTH

Not that we are sufficient of Ourselves to think of anything As being from ourselves but our Sufficiency is from GOD.

2 CORINTHIANS 3:5

Our creator God is our source;
Being employed is a resource.
Apart from the Lord
Nothing will manifest!

Comments and Notes:

_____

_____

_____

_____

_____

Day 28

NUGGETS OF TRUTH

Righteousness exalts a nation, But sin is a reproach to any people.

PROVERBS 14:34

Living a holy and honorable
life brings the Lord honor;
However, sin is missing the mark!

Comments and Notes:

_____

_____

_____

_____

_____

_____

Day 29

NUGGETS OF TRUTH

Therefore, whether you eat or drink Or whatever you do, do it all to the glory of God.

1 CORINTHIANS 10:31

As we engage in our daily affairs;
One must be mindful of our
Heavenly Father; He knows and sees all!

Comments and Notes:

_____

_____

_____

_____

_____

_____

Day 30

NUGGETS OF TRUTH

You are our epistles written
In our hearts, known
And read by all men.

2 CORINTHIANS 3:2

Living in this world means being under a microscope when we name Jesus as our Savior. One must be a walking, humble, and obedient bible.

Comments and Notes:

_____

_____

_____

_____

_____

Day 31

NUGGETS OF TRUTH

For our boasting is this:
The testimony of our conscience
That we conducted ourselves
In the world
In simplicity and godly sincerity,
Not with fleshly wisdom
But by the grace of God,
And more abundantly toward you.

2 CORINTHIANS 1:12 –AMP

We must not boast in ourselves;
For it is the Holy Spirit that is our
Helper, keeper, and guide.

Comments and Notes:

Day 32

NUGGETS OF TRUTH

Beloved, do not imitate what is evil,
But what is good.
He who does good is of God,
But he who does evil has not seen God.

3 JOHN 11

As being a child of God;
One must cling to what is good
And run from the very presence of evil!

Comments and Notes:

_____

_____

_____

Day 33

NUGGETS OF TRUTH

For God is my witness, whom I serve with my spirit in the gospel Of His Son, that without ceasing I make mention of you always in my prayers.

ROMANS 1:9

The Lord knows our every action;
As we spent time with Him in prayer;
One may encourage others as the need arises.

Comments and Notes:

_____

_____

_____

_____

Day 34

NUGGETS OF TRUTH

Beloved, I pray that you may
Prosper in all things
And be in health,
Just as you soul prospers.

3 JOHN 2

Father God is concerned about us;
Especially that we walk in divine
Health and healing; then our
Entire being will increase!

Comments and Notes:

_____

_____

_____

_____

Day 35

NUGGETS OF TRUTH

Who also made us sufficient as Ministers of the new covenant, Not of the Letter but of the Spirit, For the letter kills, but the Spirit Gives life.

2 CORINTHIANS 3:6

The word of the Lord is truth;
Jesus gave us a better covenant;
With more excellent promises;
In the past the letter of the law
Brought death, but the Holy
Spirit gives us life through the word of God!!!

Comments and Notes:

_____

_____

_____

Day 36

NUGGETS OF TRUTH

Blessed be the God and Father Of our Lord Jesus Christ, Who has blessed us with Every spiritual blessing in the Heavenly places in Christ.

EPHESIANS 1:3

Let us give the Lord thanks in all Things, He has given us all Good and perfect gifts from heaven.

Comments and Notes:

_____

_____

_____

_____

Day 37

NUGGETS OF TRUTH

For what if some did not believe? Will their unbelief make the faithfulness Of God without effect? Certainly not! Indeed, let God be True but every man a liar. As it is Written: "That you may be justified In your words, And may overcome when You are judged."

ROMANS 3:3-4

We must continue in the things of God;
For He is the truth; whether people
Believe or not. His very character is Agape Love.
One is justified because of His grace!!!

Comments and Notes:

Day 38

NUGGETS OF TRUTH

*For all have sinned
And fall short of the
Glory of God.*

ROMANS 3:23

**Every one of us was born into sin;
The sacrifice of Jesus shed blood redeemed us.**

Comments and Notes:

Day 39

NUGGETS OF TRUTH

All Scripture is given by the Inspiration of God, and is profitable For doctrine, for reproof, for Correction, for instructions in Righteousness, that the man of God May be complete Thoroughly Equipped for every Good work.

2 TIMOTHY 3:16-17

The Bible was written for our example,
Admonition, it is beneficial for
Spiritual growth as well as conducting
The affairs of this life.

Comments and Notes:

Day 40

NUGGETS OF TRUTH

*Being confident of this very thing,
That He who begun a good
Work in you will complete
It until the day of Jesus Christ.*

PHILIPPIANS 1:6

One must realize that God has
A purpose and plan for our lives;
Walking in His obedience brings completion!

Comments and Notes:

Day 41

NUGGETS OF TRUTH

Let bitterness, wrath, anger, Clamor, and evil speaking be put Away from you, With all malice.

EPHESIANS 4:31

One must avoid being angry all the times;
Also, being careful of the words that we speak.
We will be judged by our words.

Comments and Notes:

_____

_____

_____

_____

Day 42

NUGGETS OF TRUTH

Yes, all who desire to live Godly in Christ will Suffer persecution.

2 TIMOTHY 3:12

Godly living and being Christians
Will cause us many sorrows
But the Lord will wipe the tears
From our eyes and vindicate us.

Comments and Notes:

Day 43

NUGGETS OF TRUTH

*For I am not ashamed
Of the gospel of Christ,
For it is the power of
God to salvation
For everyone who believes,
For the Jew first and also
The Greek.*

ROMANS 1:16

One must stand up for the good news
Of Jesus Christ; while not compromising
Our relationship with Him; by doing so
We may receive salvation and enjoy
Eternal life in heaven.

Comments and Notes:

Day 44

NUGGETS OF TRUTH

*Be sober, be vigilant,
Because your adversary the devil
Walks about like a roaring lion,
Seeking whom he may devour.*

1 PETER 5:8

**As we remain alert in these end
Times, the enemy or false prophets
Will not deceive or destroy us.**

Comments and Notes:

Day 45

NUGGETS OF TRUTH

And they took offense at Him (they were repelled and hindered from acknowledging His authority, and caused to stumble). But Jesus said to them, a prophet is not without Honor except in his own country And in his own house.

MATTHEW 13:57 - AMP

At times one may not be recognized
Because of the anointing that is on our life,
But others outside of our sanctuary will
Appreciate and acknowledge the gift.
You must become comfortable in the
Gifts that God imparts- he anoints the call!!

Comments and Notes:

Day 46

NUGGETS OF TRUTH

Repent (think differently; Change your mind, regretting your Sins and changing your conduct), For the kingdom of heaven Is at hand.

MATTHEW 3:2 - AMP

John the Baptist reminded others
That one must be Godly sorrowful
Because of willful sin; the Lord is
Coming back soon for spotless church!!

Comments and Notes:

_____

_____

_____

_____

Day 47

NUGGETS OF TRUTH

Withstand him; be firm in faith (against his Onset – rooted, established, strong, immovable, And determined), knowing that the same (identical) sufferings are appointed to your brotherhood (the whole body of Christians) throughout the world.

1 PETER 5:9 - AMP

While no one enjoys trials or tribulations
One can rest assured that our brothers
Are experiencing the same things-
The enemy will have us to believe
That we are the only ones that are having
Challenges in our life.
His tactics are exposed and he is a liar.

Comments and Notes:

Day 48

NUGGETS OF TRUTH

It is written:
Man shall not live by bread alone,
But by every word that proceeds
From the mouth of God.

MATTHEW 4:4

Our life must consist of studying and Meditating of God's word daily.

Comments and Notes:

_____

_____

_____

_____

_____

_____

Day 49

NUGGETS OF TRUTH

For this reason I bow my knees
To the Father
of our Lord Jesus Christ;
From whom the whole family
In heaven and earth is named.

EPHESIANS 3:14-15

There will come a day when every knee
Will bow and every tongue shall confess
the sovereignty of our Holy God.

Comments and Notes:

_____

_____

_____

_____

Day 50

NUGGETS OF TRUTH

*For we are His workmanship,
Created in Christ Jesus
For good works,
Which God prepared beforehand
That we should walk in them.*

EPHESIANS 2:10

**All human flesh is the Lord's creative work,
Woven and ingrained like tapestry but
Washed in the blood of the Lamb.**

Comments and Notes:

_____

_____

_____

_____

Day 51

NUGGETS OF TRUTH

For who is the greater, the one who Reclines at the table (the master), Or the one who serves? Is it not the One who reclines at the table? But I am in the midst as One who serves.

LUKE 22:27 - AMP

Jesus set the example
Of humility by serving at all times.
When one shows humility this
Opens doors of divine opportunities.

Comments and Notes:

_____

_____

_____

Day 52

NUGGETS OF TRUTH

If I then, your Lord and teacher (Master) have washed your feet, You ought (it is your duty, you are Under obligation, you owe it) to Wash one another's feet.

JOHN 13:14 - AMP

Showing love for your neighbor includes girding Up one's self by washing feet.

Comments and Notes:

Day 53

NUGGETS OF TRUTH

But stripped Himself
(of all privileges
And rightful dignity),
So as to assume the guise of a
servant (slave)
In that He became like men
And was born a human being.

PHILIPPIANS 2: 7

What are you willing to give up
To follow Christ example?
Serving brings honor,
humility of Spirit and freedom.

Comments and Notes:

Day 54

NUGGETS OF TRUTH

Just as the Son of Man came
Not to be waited on
But to serve,
And to give His life as a ransom
For many
(the price paid to set them free).

MATTHEW 20:28 - AMP

Being a servant is a great asset
In the kingdom of God and brings lasting benefits.

Comments and Notes:

_____

_____

_____

_____

Day 55

NUGGETS OF TRUTH

For there is one
God and one Mediator
Between God and men,
The Man Christ Jesus.
Who gave Himself a ransom
For all, to be testified in due time.

1 TIMOTHY 2:5-6

Realize this truth one can only receive from
God through Jesus Christ.
There's no other way!!

Comments and Notes:

_____

_____

_____

Day 56

NUGGETS OF TRUTH

Jesus said to them,
My food (nourishment)
Is to do the will (pleasure) of Him
Who sent Me and to accomplish
And completely finish
His work.

JOHN 4:34 - AMP

A good teacher gives assignments
on a regular basis;
To measure the level of knowledge
that students gain.

Comments and Notes:

_____

_____

_____

Day 57

NUGGETS OF TRUTH

Hear O Israel; The LORD our God The Lord is one!

DEUTERONOMY 6:4

Now, as one engages in prayer and worship,
On a daily basis our spirit man will come
Into proper alignment.

Comments and Notes:

_____

_____

_____

_____

_____

_____

Day 58

NUGGETS OF TRUTH

He did not do many mighty works There because of their unbelief.

MATTHEW 13:58

A person can't confess belief and doubt
In the same breath. Unbelief is a destroyer of faith.
It is impossible for them
To co-exist at the same time.
Can you locate yourself?

Comments and Notes:

Day 59

NUGGETS OF TRUTH

*And the love of the great body
Of people will grow cold
Because of the multiplied lawlessness.*

MATTHEW 24:12 - AMP

Unfortunately, people are losing focus on our creator
By turning their backs on God in order
To satisfy lustful deeds!

Comments and Notes:

_____

_____

_____

_____

Day 60

NUGGETS OF TRUTH

*And this good news
Of the kingdom (The Gospel)
Will be preached throughout
The whole world as a testimony
To all the nations, and
Then the end will come.*

MATTHEW 24:14 - AMP

There is hope for helpless, hopeless and hurting
People because of the Lord's
Goodness, mercy and grace.
Salvation is available to everyone
Before judgment comes.

Comments and Notes:

_____

_____

Day 61

NUGGETS OF TRUTH

*For as lightening come out
Of the east, and shine even unto
The west so shall the coming
Of the Son of man be.*

MATTHEW 24:27

God's Word gives off light
In dark areas in our lives.
Be alert the Lord is soon to return.

Comments and Notes:

_____

_____

_____

_____

Day 62

NUGGETS OF TRUTH

Heaven and earth shall away,
But my words shall not pass away.

MATTHEW 24:35

The entire world's system will be destroyed,
But the WORD of the Lord
Will remain forever.

Comments and Notes:

_____

_____

_____

_____

_____

_____

Day 63

NUGGETS OF TRUTH

Paul, an apostle (special messenger Appointed commissioned and sent Out) not from (any body of) men Nor by or Through any man, but by And through Jesus Christ (the Messiah) and God the Father, Who raised him from the dead.

GALATIANS 1:1 - AMP

There are countless men and women
That have been
Anointed, commissioned and appointed
To be a testimony in the earth.
Are you one?

Comments and Notes:

Day 64

NUGGETS OF TRUTH

*But when it pleased God,
Who separated me from my
mother's womb
And called me through His grace.*

GALATIANS 1:15

Some persons have been called, chosen from
Their birth to walk in divine Favor.
Will you accept your call?

Comments and Notes:

_____

_____

_____

_____

_____

Day 65

NUGGETS OF TRUTH

Do not be deceived, and deluded and Misled; God will not allow Himself to Be sneered at (scorned, disdained, or Mocked by mere pretensions or Professions, or by His precepts being set aside.) (He inevitably deludes himself who attempts to delude God.) For whatever a man sows, that and that only is what he will reap.

Galatians 6:7 - Amp

People will mislead us if one allows it – The seeds that we have sown will return a harvest after its own kind. What kind of garden are you growing?

Comments and Notes:

Day 66

NUGGETS OF TRUTH

Bear (endure, carry) one another's Burdens and troublesome moral faults, and in this way fulfill and observe perfectly The law of Christ (the Messiah) and complete what is lacking (In your obedience to it.)

GALATIANS 6:2 - AMP

One must be concerned with our peer's trials –
Because we are our brothers
Or sisters keepers.

Comments and Notes:

_____

_____

_____

Day 67

NUGGETS OF TRUTH

For if anyone person thinks himself To be somebody (too important to condescend to shoulder another's load) when he is nobody (of superiority except in his own estimation), he deceives and deludes and cheats himself.

GALATIANS 6:3 - AMP

It is vital that a person displays a mild,
Meek and humble spirit at all times
Otherwise they may stumble and fall
While landing on prides platform!

Comments and Notes:

Day 68

NUGGETS OF TRUTH

*Let this mind be in you,
Which was also in Christ Jesus;
Whom being in the form of God,
Thought it not robbery
to be equal with God.*

Philippians 2: 5-6

Our mindset must reflect our Elder Brother Jesus, The author and processor of our Faith!

Comments and Notes:

_____

_____

_____

_____

Day 69

NUGGETS OF TRUTH

*But made Himself of no reputation,
And took upon him the form
Of a servant, and was made
In the likeness of men.*

PHILIPPIANS 2:7

There needs to be transparency
When one is preaching, teaching, serving
And walking out daily assignments.
Jesus left us an example to follow.

Comments and Notes:

_____

_____

_____

_____

_____

Day 70

NUGGETS OF TRUTH

If possible,
As far as it depends on you,
Live at peace with everyone.

ROMANS 12:18 - AMP

Living on this earth in a tranquil state is possible. How? When we reflect on the very Character, nature and heartbeat of God!! By dispersing peace like a dove.

Comments and Notes:

Day 71

NUGGETS OF TRUTH

Let every person be loyally subjected
To the governing (civil) authorities.
For there is no authority
Except from God (by His sanction),
And those that exists do so by God's appointment.

ROMANS 13:1- AMP

Similarly, it is important that we comply
To governing officials because that is sanctioned
By God – he permits it!

Comments and Notes:

_____

_____

_____

Day 72

NUGGETS OF TRUTH

*Your ears shall hear
A word behind you, saying
"This is the way, walk in it"
Whenever you turn to the
Right hand or whenever you
Turn to the left.*

ISAIAH 30:21

Pay attention, listen and hear
With your spiritual ears.
Next, follow instructions
Without wavering in the Faith.
Can you stop and listen for one minute?

Comments and Notes:

Day 73

NUGGETS OF TRUTH

In You O LORD,
I put my trust,
Let me never be ashamed;
Deliver me in your righteousness.

PSALM 31:1

Now, as we put our total confidence
And allegiance in God – there shouldn't
Be any embarrassment; just sweat less victory
And uprightness in Him!

Comments and Notes:

Day 74

NUGGETS OF TRUTH

*I give you a new commandment:
That you should love one another.
Just as I have loved you,
So you too should love one another.*

JOHN 13:34 - AMP

God compels us to live a life of loving each other,
Because he instituted Agape Love
By loving us first.
Will you chose to Love on purpose?

Comments and Notes:

_____

_____

_____

_____

_____

Day 75

NUGGETS OF TRUTH

*By this shall all (men) know
That you are My disciples,
If you love one another
(If you keep on showing love
Among yourselves).*

JOHN 13:35 - AMP

A witness to mankind can be seen in followers
Of Jesus Christ – while one is displaying
The garment of love to each other!

Comments and Notes:

_____

_____

_____

_____

Day 76

NUGGETS OF TRUTH

Nevertheless I have this Against you, that you have left your first love.

REVELATION 2:4

One should never lose their Sacred first Love By replacing Jesus with earthly possessions. Jesus Love is ANOINTED, selfless, and eternal!!!

Comments and Notes:

Day 77

NUGGETS OF TRUTH

But you are a chosen generation,
A royal priesthood, a holy nation.
His own special people, that you
May proclaim the praises
Of Him who called you out
Of darkness into His marvelous light.

1 PETER 2:9

People that are sanctified (set-apart)
As heirs for Jesus Christ must
Live a life of holiness; with grateful hearts
Of adoration for being snatched from the pit of sin
And ushered into the glorious brilliance
Of celestial lights.

Comments and Notes:

_____

_____

Day 78

NUGGETS OF TRUTH

Bow down your ear to me,
Deliver me speedily;
Be my rock of refuge,
A fortress of defense to save me.

PSALM 31:2

In the condition of this world
One can escape the trap that is laid
Up by our enemies; by running into God's protection!

Comments and Notes:

_____

_____

_____

_____

_____

Day 79

NUGGETS OF TRUTH

My times are in Your hands:
Deliver me from the hand
Of my enemies,
And those who persecute me.

PSALM 31:15

Lord there's no other place of deliverance
Other than, under the shadow of the most high.
Is there any other place of protection?

Comments and Notes:

Day 80

NUGGETS OF TRUTH

I am forgotten like a dead man,
Out of mind;
I am like a broken vessel.

PSALM 31:12

In this world without Christ One is lifeless,
Non-living; as a broken bone out of joint
Or marred like shattered pottery.
Are you walking around breathless like a corpse?

Comments and Notes:

_____

_____

_____

_____

_____

Day 81

NUGGETS OF TRUTH

Man that is born of a woman
Is of a few days and full of trouble.

JOB 14:1

Our natural birth was painful
And can be shortened with calamity,
Destruction, diseases, trials and tribulations.
But our spiritual birth can sustain us.

Comments and Notes:

_____

_____

_____

_____

_____

_____

Day 82

NUGGETS OF TRUTH

For His anger is but for a moment,
But His favor is for a lifetime;
Or in His favor is life.
Weeping may endure for a night,
But joy Comes in the morning.

PSALM 30:5 - AMP

While one is out of the will of God,
His wrath can be swift, but our creator's
Grace is everlasting. Then, joy is released –
In the dawn of the day.

Comments and Notes:

_____

_____

_____

_____

Day 83

NUGGETS OF TRUTH

*He comes forth like a flower
And withers; He flees also
Like a shadow and continues not.*

JOB 14:2 - AMP

Life is passing us by like peddles
Falling from flowers and dies;
Shadows are here one day and vanishes
The next as light appears.

Comments and Notes:

Day 84

NUGGETS OF TRUTH

*Though He slay me,
Yet will I trust Him.
Even so, I will defend
My own ways Before Him.*

JOB 13:15

While fiery darts come to test and try our faith,
We must still rely on and have confidence in God.
Will you trust Him in the STORMS?

Comments and Notes:

_____

_____

_____

_____

_____

Day 85

NUGGETS OF TRUTH

With Him is wisdom and strength, He has counsel and understanding.

JOB 12:13

One may gain skillful and Godly Wisdom; This brings strength, while His counsel Releases understanding, discernment, Comprehension and interpretation.

Comments and Notes:

Day 86

NUGGETS OF TRUTH

He said to them, because of the littleness of your faith (that is your lack of firmly relying trust). For truly I say to you if you have faith (that is living) like a grain of mustard seed, you can say to this mountain, move from here to yonder place, and it will move; and nothing will be impossible to you.

MATTHEW 17:20 - AMP

Our faith must mature from the mustard seed
To great faith by conveying God's word
Doing so brings limitless possibilities!

Comments and Notes:

Day 87

NUGGETS OF TRUTH

*Make a joyful noise unto the Lord,
All the earth; make a loud noise,
And rejoice and sing praise.*

PSALM 98:4

Sing to God new songs,
From the inner most depths of your spirit.
Everything should be done for His glory!

Comments and Notes:

Day 88

NUGGETS OF TRUTH

*This beginning of signs
Jesus did in Cana of Galilee,
And manifested forth His glory,
And His disciples believed in Him.*

JOHN 2:11

From start to finish our Christ
Did as the Father instructed Him to do.
As followers of Jesus we must
believe, receive and obey!
Are you fully persuaded in Him?

Comments and Notes:

_____

_____

_____

_____

Day 89

NUGGETS OF TRUTH

Nathanael answered him, (Nazareth!) Can anything good come Out of Nazareth? Phillip replied, come and see!

JOHN 1:46 - AMP

Regardless what people convey about you
With Jesus Christ as our Lord and Savior
One's location can flourish; whether city,
County or state all can be blessed because of you!
Your character and lifestyle is important!

Comments and Notes:

_____

_____

_____

Day 90

NUGGETS OF TRUTH

Set your mind on things above,
Not of things on the earth.

COLOSSIANS 3:2

We must think of heavenly promises
They are guaranteed, tried, proven
Protected and manifested!
Are your thoughts on the kingdom of God?
Or gaining more material wealth?

Comments and Notes:

_____

_____

_____

_____

_____

_____

Day 91

NUGGETS OF TRUTH

For (as far as this world is concerned) You have died, And your (new real) life Is hidden with Christ in God.

COLOSSIANS 3:3

The new birth brings spiritual life
Our old man should not be on the throne
(no longer lives). The real person
is hid from the world in Jesus Christ!
Does your image reflect Jesus?

Comments and Notes:

_____

_____

_____

_____

Day 92

NUGGETS OF TRUTH

And whatever you do,
Do it heartily, as to the Lord
And not to men.

COLOSSIANS 3:23

All that we pursue, task, assignments,
Vocation, and play should be done
With excellence and from the heart
Giving all the glory to the Lord!
Is the Lord pleased with your works?

Comments and Notes:

_____

_____

_____

_____

_____

Day 93

NUGGETS OF TRUTH

Continue earnestly in prayer. Being vigilant in it with thanksgiving.

COLOSSIANS 4:2

Always pray constantly without reservation,
Being alert and watchful giving thanks
To His name; prayer is a weighty
Matter, promises and assurance!
When your prayers are not answered quickly
Do you stop praying?

Comments and Notes:

Day 94

NUGGETS OF TRUTH

For in Christ Jesus neither Circumcision (now) of any importance, Nor uncircumcision, but (only) a new creation (The results of a new birth and a new Nature in Christ Jesus, the Messiah)

GALATIANS 6:15

A person that has accepted Jesus Christ Is given a fresh start (new beginnings) This is called the new birth. Are you born again? If not, what are you waiting for?

Comments and Notes:

_____

_____

_____

Day 95

NUGGETS OF TRUTH

Let your speech always be with grace, Seasoned with salt, that you may Know how you ought to Answer each one.

COLOSSIANS 4:6

You must be cautious of the words that one speaks,
For they can be pleasant to the palate
Or leave a bitter after taste.

Comments and Notes:

Day 96

NUGGETS OF TRUTH

*For you were brought with a price
Therefore glorify God in
Your body and in your spirit,
Which are God's?*

1 CORINTHIANS 6:20

Being in God's family is priceless!
Therefore we must not abuse our bodies,
Because our spirit belongs to Jesus.
Treat it with loving Care!

Comments and Notes:

Day 97

NUGGETS OF TRUTH

At the same time pray for us also, That God may open a door to us For the Word, (the Gospel) to proclaim The mystery concerning Christ (the Messiah) on account Of which I am in prison; That I may proclaim it fully and make It clear (speak boldly and unfold That mystery), as is my duty.

COLOSSIANS 4:3-4 - AMP

There are doors of opportunity to minister The Word of God. However, our main focus should be on Him – Not on us. Sometimes it may Seem as if we are confined! And rightfully so, because this platform is for His glory! Selah!

Comments and Notes:

Day 98

NUGGETS OF TRUTH

Flee sexual immorality
Every sin that a man does is outside
The body, but he who commits
sexual Immortality sins against his
own body.

1 CORINTHIANS 6:18

Selfish sexual desires toward our bodies is sin;
This should be avoided. One can't hide,
From God, He sees it all!

Comments and Notes:
_____
_____
_____
_____

Day 99

NUGGETS OF TRUTH

For where two or three are gathered In My name, I am in the midst of them.

MATTHEW 18:20

The Lord is present when we come together
To pray or assemble in Jesus name!
When was the last time that the Lord visited you?
Selah!

Comments and Notes:

_____

_____

_____

_____

_____

Day 100

NUGGETS OF TRUTH

We are fools for Christ sake, But you are wise in Christ! We are weak, But you are strong! You are distinguished, But we are dishonored.

1 CORINTHIANS 4:10

Some people may be ashamed of the Gospel
Of Jesus Christ; this may appear foolish
To the world, but for the one who stands up
Will be given strength, power, grace
And honor in His name!
Hallelujah!

Comments and Notes:

_____

_____

Day 101

NUGGETS OF TRUTH

That which is born of the flesh Is flesh, and that which is born Of the Spirit is spirit.

JOHN 3:6

Our natural birth is from the flesh
Of two persons, ones parents.
But when we receive Jesus as Lord;
This is a spiritual birth!
Selah!

Comments and Notes:

Day 102

NUGGETS OF TRUTH

*Your Faithfulness endures
to all generations;
You established the earth,
and it abides.*

PSALM 119:90

The Lords attributes are final
From the beginning when the earth was formed;
Until the end of time His faith is everlasting
from one generation to the next.

Comments and Notes:

_____

_____

_____

_____

_____

Day 103

NUGGETS OF TRUTH

*How sweet are Your Words
To my taste, sweeter than honey to
my mouth!*

PSALM 119:103

God's Words are sweeter to our spirit;
Its taste is more delicious than honey to a bee!
Have you ever tasted God's word?

Comments and Notes:

_____

_____

_____

_____

_____

Day 104

NUGGETS OF TRUTH

*He must increase,
but I must decrease.*

JOHN 3:30

Whatever one does
It should always reflect on the Lord first.
Our attitude and all that we possess
Must bow in the presence of our King!
Glory, Glory!

Comments and Notes:

_____

_____

_____

_____

_____

Day 105

Nuggets of Truth

So then those who are of Faith Are blessed with believing Abraham.

Galatians 3:9

Abraham is the Father of Faith.
Those who believe in and adhere to faithful
Teachings are blessed because of Him!
Are you in the family of faith or doubt?

Comments and Notes:

Day 106

NUGGETS OF TRUTH

But Scripture has confined all under sin that the promise by Faith in Jesus Christ might be given to those who believe.

GALATIANS 3:22

The law demanded righteousness
But proved powerless to provide it
But we have Faith in Jesus
Christ the second Adam;
The one who is sinless!

Comments and Notes:

_____

_____

_____

_____

Day 107

Nuggets of Truth

*And we labor,
working with our own hands.
Being reviled, we bless,
Being persecuted, we endure.*

1 Corinthians 4:12

In all labor there is profit,
Then if one is persecuted, God blesses us
And gives us His grace for endurance.

Comments and Notes:

Day 108

NUGGETS OF TRUTH

*But before faith came, we were kept
Under guard by the law,
Kept for the faith which would
Afterward be revealed.*

GALATIANS 3:23

The law kept us bound as in chains;
Watching a person's every move.
But Faith has delivered us and our promises
Are clear like an image in a mirror.   Selah!

Comments and Notes:

_____

_____

_____

_____

_____

Day 109

NUGGETS OF TRUTH

Love your enemies, do good And lend hoping for nothing in return.

LUKE 6:35

As we love those who mean us harm;
One is extending compassion,
As we keep the peace
Our reward is coming from the Lord!
Hallelujah!

Comments and Notes:

_____

_____

_____

_____

_____

Day 110

NUGGETS OF TRUTH

*So then faith comes by hearing,
And hearing by the word of God.*

ROMANS 10:17

Reading the word out loud, and meditating
On the promises of God regularly
Will cause your faith to become
Activated and alive!
What are you listening to?

Comments and Notes:

_____

_____

_____

_____

_____

_____

Day 111

NUGGETS OF TRUTH

*Bless those who curse you,
And pray for those who spitefully use you.*

LUKE 6:28

It is the Holy Spirit that enables us
To choose on purpose to be a blessing
For people who wrong us and by praying for them.
How long has it been that you spoke a blessing
Over an enemy?

Comments and Notes:

_____

_____

_____

_____

_____

Day 112

NUGGETS OF TRUTH

I have not come to call the righteous, But sinners, to repentance.

LUKE 5:32

Jesus is concerned about unbelievers
Who do not know Him, He desires for them
To repent and receive Him as Lord!
After all, He gave us an opportunity!
How many people have you led to Jesus Christ?

Comments and Notes:

_____

_____

_____

_____

Day 113

NUGGETS OF TRUTH

And if you do good to those who do Good to you, what credit is that to you?
For even sinners do the same.

LUKE 6:33

One must reach out to all persons.
Yes, even the ones that falsely accuse us
Or even mistreat us
Jesus set the example, can we follow Him?

Comments and Notes:

_____

_____

_____

_____

_____

Day 114

NUGGETS OF TRUTH

Servants, be submissive to your
Masters with all fear,
Not only to the good
And gentle, but also to the harsh.

1 PETER 2:18

The Lord needs us to be diligent in our work ethnics
Even if our employers are kind or abrasive.
He allows them to possess their positions
So, one must give the respect that is due.
If one is mistreated the Lord will vindicate us!

Comments and Notes:

_____

_____

_____

_____

Day 115

NUGGETS OF TRUTH

*Therefore be merciful,
Just as you Father also is merciful.*

LUKE 6:36

The entire human race deserves being shown kindness, compassion and courteous as the next person regardless of their lot in life.
When will you stop showing partiality?

Comments and Notes:

Day 116

NUGGETS OF TRUTH

For you are all sons of God Through faith in Christ Jesus.

GALATIANS 3:26

A person does not become a Son
until he/she accepts Jesus as Lord
Salvation is received by confession of our
Faith in the Lord Jesus Christ.
Are you a son or daughter yet?

Comments and Notes:

_____

_____

_____

_____

_____

Day 117

NUGGETS OF TRUTH

Forever, O LORD,
Your word is settled in heaven.

PSALM 119:89

One must resolve the issue of God's word
For eternity, it is established in the heavens.
Therefore, we must be carriers on the earth!
Thank you Jesus!

Comments and Notes:

_____

_____

_____

_____

_____

Day 118

NUGGETS OF TRUTH

Therefore the law was our tutor,
To bring us to Christ,
That we might be justified by faith.

GALATIANS 3:24

The law gave us limitations
In Jesus Christ we are declared and made
Righteous through Faith in Him alone!
What a Blessed Assurance from the Lord!

Comments and Notes:

_____

_____

_____

_____

_____

_____

Day 119

NUGGETS OF TRUTH

*But as for you,
you meant evil against Me;
but God meant it for good,
in order to bring it about as it is this
day, to save many people alive.*

GENESIS 50:20

Sometimes people may plan plot, scheme
Or fabricate lies, even mischief but the Lord will
Vindicate us and bring safety to many because
Of our peace and long suffering!
Don't be fooled or tricked by the enemy.
He is not your friend!

Comments and Notes:

_____

_____

_____

Day 120

NUGGETS OF TRUTH

*For this is commendable,
If because of conscience toward God
One endures grief, suffering
wrongfully.*

1 PETER 2:19

**Abba Father honors the suffering and persecutions
That one endures because of Him;
He shall make the crooked places straight.**

Comments and Notes:

_____

_____

_____

_____

_____

Day 121

NUGGETS OF TRUTH

The Lord is far from the wicked, But He hears the prayer of the righteous.

PROVERBS 15: 29

A person who practices willful sin,
While living a corrupt lifestyle
Will not be heard by God.
Don't be naïve to think that God answered
Your prayer if this is your lifestyle.
He answers the prayers of the righteous!

Comments and Notes:

Day 122

Nuggets of Truth

For as many of you were baptized into Christ Have put on Christ.

Galatians 3:27

Clothing oneself with Christ likeness Conveys you are in covenant with Him. Do you have on your garment?

Comments and Notes:

Day 123

NUGGETS OF TRUTH

God resist the proud,
But gives grace to the humble.

1 PETER 5:5B

Let us avoid boasting in ourselves
The humble in spirit will receive
God's favor for a lifetime.
Where do you fit, proud of humble?
You decide your fate.

Comments and Notes:

Day 124

NUGGETS OF TRUTH

*But let all those who take refuge and
Put their trust in You rejoice,
Let them ever sing and shout for joy,
Because You make a covering over
Them and defend them,
Let those also who love Your name
Be joyful in You and be in high
Spirits.*

PSALM 5:11- AMP

Run into the arms of Jesus
As one trust Him in all things
He promised to defend, protect and we will praise Him!

Comments and Notes:

Day 125

NUGGETS OF TRUTH

Do two walk together except
They make an appointment
And have agreed?

AMOS 3:3 -AMP

In a covenant relationship two parties
Must agree to go in the same direction
Especially in marriage, worship and Christianity!

Comments and Notes:

Day 126

NUGGETS OF TRUTH

*If you willing and obedient
You shall eat the good of the land.*

ISAIAH 1:19 - AMP

In life sometimes persons are willing to change,
But they have trouble obeying new directions of
actions; For the blessings of the Lord to invade our
Very being, then both of these actions must be
Evident in our life. They are inseparable.
This is a two-fold promise!

Comments and Notes:

Day 127

NUGGETS OF TRUTH

Keep on asking and it will be given;
Keep on seeking and you will find;
Keep on knocking (reverently)
And (the door) will be opened.

MATTHEW 7:7 -AMP

One must keep asking, seeking, and knocking
In order to receive the promises of God
That is behind the Word!
Mix the word with Faith no doubting allowed!

Comments and Notes:

Day 128

NUGGETS OF TRUTH

*Jesus Christ (the Messiah)
is (always) the same,
Yesterday, today,
(yes) and forever
(to the ages).*

HEBREWS 13:8 - AMP

In the beginning was Jesus the Anointed One,
Constantly unchanging full of mercy, grace
Truth and Loving kindness from now to eternity.

Comments and Notes:

_____

_____

_____

_____

Day 129

NUGGETS OF TRUTH

But seek (aim at and strive after)
First of all His kingdom
and His righteousness
(His way of doing and being right),
And then all these things taken
together will be even you besides.

MATTHEW 6:33 - AMP

One needs to go after God and His righteousness,
Being right and in right standing with Him
For then all our needs shall be met!
Who or what are you aiming for?

Comments and Notes:

_____

_____

_____

Day 130

NUGGETS OF TRUTH

*The mind of the righteous
Studies how to answer,
But the mouth of the wicked pours
Out evil things.*

PROVERBS 15:28

Watch how you answer every question
That's asked of you. Why? Because without morals
One can have loose lips with evil pouring out!
What is coming out of your mouth?

Comments and Notes:

_____

_____

_____

_____

_____

Day 131

NUGGETS OF TRUTH

*A word fitly spoken
And in due season
is like apples of gold;
In settings of silver.*

PROVERBS 25:11- AMP

A due season Word is elegant,
Polished, crisp light and airy
Primarily, immersed in Godly wisdom and knowledge!

Comments and Notes:

_____

_____

_____

_____

Day 132

NUGGETS OF TRUTH

*Be diligent to know
the state of your flocks,
And attend to your herbs;
For riches are not forever,
Nor does a crown endure to all
generations.*

PROVERBS 27:23-24

It is imperative to know the value of your worth
But more important is your Eternal Salvation.
Will your generation know the Living Savior?

Comments and Notes:

_____

_____

_____

Day 133

NUGGETS OF TRUTH

*Open rebuke is better
Than love carefully concealed.*

PROVERBS 27:5

Speak the truth at all times
Even when it is not popular or welcomed.
By doing this it shows Love!
Convey the truth to me even if it's painful!

Comments and Notes:

_____

_____

_____

_____

_____

_____

Day 134

NUGGETS OF TRUTH

*Do not boast about tomorrow,
For you do not know what a day
May bring forth.*

PROVERBS 27:1

One should live one day at a time
Because the next day is not promised to us.
Let's rejoice in today!

Comments and Notes:

_____

_____

_____

_____

_____

Day 135

NUGGETS OF TRUTH

*Let another man praise you,
and not your own mouth;
A stranger and not your own lips.*

PROVERBS 27:2

The Lord is aware of the kindness and generosity
That we display toward His people
While man may not recognize our deeds
The Lord will reveal this to others
He will be glorified through it!

Comments and Notes:

_____

_____

_____

_____

Day 136

NUGGETS OF TRUTH

As iron sharpens iron;
So a man sharpens the countenance
Of his friend.

PROVERBS 27:17

One's friendship should be solid in nature
As steel that is liken to a railroad track,
That bears up under extreme weights.
Are you sharp or dull toward your friends?

Comments and Notes:

Day 137

Nuggets of Truth

As in water face reflects face,
So a man's heart reveals the man.

Proverbs 27:19

Your heart can speak volumes
Loud and clear without ever opening
One's lips by your actions.
Now transparency will be seen by all.

Comments and Notes:

Day 138

NUGGETS OF TRUTH

Hell and destruction are never full; So the eyes of man are never satisfied.

PROVERBS 27:20

What profits a person to gain material wealth
But forfeits his eternal soul by going to hell?
His mouth enlarges itself
always ready for more souls!
Will you ever have enough or be content?
Selah!

Comments and Notes:

_____

_____

_____

_____

_____

Day 139

NUGGETS OF TRUTH

*The wicked flee when no one pursues;
But the righteous are bold as a lion.*

PROVERBS 28:1

A person that is in right standing with the Lord,
Can stand up fearless in the face of adversity!
"There is no fear here!"

Comments and Notes:

Day 140

NUGGETS OF TRUTH

Evil men do not understand justice, But those who seek the LORD Understands all.

PROVERBS 28:5

As one pursue God he will have
Supreme Godly wisdom and understanding
However, the wicked are baffle by this.

Comments and Notes:

_____

_____

_____

_____

_____

_____

Day 141

NUGGETS OF TRUTH

Better is the poor who walks in his integrity
Than one perverse in his ways
Though he be rich.

PROVERBS 28:6

It is far better for a righteous person to
Remain humble, honest than a person
With unacceptable morals.
God sees it all!
Hallelujah!

Comments and Notes:

_____

_____

_____

_____

Day 142

NUGGETS OF TRUTH

The LORD will perfect that which Concerns me; Your mercy, O LORD, endures forever,
Do not forsake the works of Your hands.

PSALM 138:8

There's no need for alarm when it comes
To the Lord's timing; His divine will, purpose,
And favor shapes our lives and character.
The Lord finishes what He starts in us!

Comments and Notes:

_____

_____

_____

_____

Day 143

NUGGETS OF TRUTH

O LORD, you have searched me and known me.
You know my sitting down and my Rising up; You understand my thought afar off.

PSALM 139:1-2

Our creator has been seeking us,
He is omnipresent so He is aware of everything
That we are engaged in from the
Sun rising in the mornings or setting in the evening
The Lord is aware of our thoughts
Before we release them!

Comments and Notes:

_____

_____

_____

Day 144

NUGGETS OF TRUTH

Where can I go from your Spirit? Or where can I flee from your presence?

PSALM 139:7

Absolutely no where can we escape
The Almighty God's presence.
He's aware of all things!
Who would even dare try?

Comments and Notes:

Day 145

NUGGETS OF TRUTH

If I ascend into heaven,
You are there;
If I make my bed in hell, behold,
You Are there.

PSALM 139:8

Abba Father has free reign in the heavens
Earth or even in hell.
You see, He took the keys from hell
And locked up the demons.
All power is in His hands!

Comments and Notes:

Day 146

NUGGETS OF TRUTH

Praise the LORD!
Praise God in His sanctuary;
Praise Him in His mighty firmament!

PSALM 150:1

Worship is what God desires of us
One must boast, rave, celebrate
with exceeding joy, shout
Of triumph, extreme praise
And dance before the Lord!
Will you join this sacred movement?

Comments and Notes:

Day 147

NUGGETS OF TRUTH

Praise Him for His mighty acts; Praise Him according to His excellent greatness!

PSALM 150:2

One must applaud, commend, honor,
Worship the Lord for who He is.
Thank you Lord, we bask in your presence!

Comments and Notes:

_____

_____

_____

_____

Day 148

NUGGETS OF TRUTH

Praise Him with the sound of the trumpet; Praise Him with the lute and harp!

PSALM 150:3

Even with our voices lifted up
they can become instruments.
One can praise and worship the Lord!

Comments and Notes:

Day 149

NUGGETS OF TRUTH

Praise Him with the tumbrel and dance; Praise Him with stringed instruments And flutes!

PSALM 150:4

One can become creative in praise
And worship with handkerchiefs
Or even flags or violins
Dancing even spinning around before the Lord!
Are you free to worship the Lord in the sanctuary?

Comments and Notes:

_____

_____

_____

_____

Day 150

NUGGETS OF TRUTH

*Praise Him with loud cymbals;
Praise Him with clashing cymbals!*

PSALM 150:5

One must not be silent when praising the Lord.
He invites the cymbals to praise.
Praise and worship is an individual act.

Comments and Notes:

_____

_____

_____

_____

_____

_____

_____

Day 151

NUGGETS OF TRUTH

Let everything that has breath Praise the LORD. Praise the LORD!

PSALM 150:6

The birds of the air chirp
The tree limbs and leaves blow
Bees release honey into honeycombs
The oceans waves beat on the shore
All of creation owes homage,
Worship and praise to God our creator!

Comments and Notes:

Day 152

NUGGETS OF TRUTH

Do not withhold good from those to whom it is due, when it is in the power of your hand
To do so.

PROVERBS 3:27

It is important to extend goodness and mercy
when you are in the position of authority
to help others do not run or dodge
from your assignment!
They don't go away, but follow you!
Selah!!!

Comments and Notes:

_____

_____

_____

_____

Day 153

Nuggets of Truth

*Do not say to your neighbor,
"Go, and come back,
And tomorrow I will give it,"
When you have it with you.*

Proverbs 3:28

There's nothing like living doing
Things that are task to us as they come.
Procrastination is a thief.
A persons blessings can be hindered
Because of disobedience.

Comments and Notes:
_____
_____
_____
_____

Day 154

NUGGETS OF TRUTH

*When you lie down,
you will not be afraid;
Yes, you will lie down
and your sleep Will be sweet.*

PROVERBS 3:24

While resting in the Lords arms
As one retires at night
Fear will not over take our thoughts
And God will give us pleasant sleep.

Comments and Notes:

_____

_____

_____

_____

Day 155

NUGGETS OF TRUTH

Ponder the path of your feet,
And let all your ways be established.
Do not turn to the right or left;
Remove your foot from evil.

PROVERBS 4: 26-27

Be careful where you go.
Pray for direction and guidance.
This will avoid snares form our enemies.
Why do you keep allowing your feet
To travel down deadly roads?

Comments and Notes:

_____

_____

_____

_____

Day 156

NUGGETS OF TRUTH

Go to the ant, you sluggard! Consider her ways and be wise, Which, having no captain, Overseer or ruler.

PROVERBS 6:6-7

One can learn from the insects.
Watch their actions and gain a wealth of wisdom!
A leader should be the first to SERVE!

Comments and Notes:

_____

_____

_____

_____

_____

Day 157

NUGGETS OF TRUTH

Provides her supplies in the summer, And gathers her food in the harvest.

PROVERBS 6:8

Plan for harvest in the summer months
By sowing seeds ahead in fertile soil!
Yes Lord, we hear and obey!

Comments and Notes:

Day 158

NUGGETS OF TRUTH

How long will you slumber, O sluggard?
When will you rise from, your sleep?

PROVERBS 6:9

Stop procrastinating and being slothful
Too much sleep will cause a person
To miss opportunities, that shapes their destiny.
Pay attention to each milestone in your life.

Comments and Notes:

Day 159

NUGGETS OF TRUTH

A little sleep, a little slumber,
A little folding of the hands to sleep.

PROVERBS 6:10

There is a time and a purpose for sleep,
But not during prayer, meditating or study of the Word of God.
This is a time for receiving from God!!!
Can you stay awake long enough to receive from God?

Comments and Notes:

_____

_____

_____

_____

_____

Day 160

NUGGETS OF TRUTH

So shall your poverty come on you
Like a prowler.
And your need like an armed man.

PROVERBS 6:11

One that doesn't have control over
Their finances can cause deficiency or lack.
Becoming poor; this spirit sneaks
Up on people, not tithing.
Will bring you to a place of drought quickly!

Comments and Notes:

Day 161

NUGGETS OF TRUTH

These six things the LORD hates, Yes, seven are an abomination to Him: A proud look, a lying tongue Hands that shed innocent blood.

PROVERBS 6:16-17

It is awful to become an enemy of God.
He detests a person, who tells lies,
People that shed innocent blood.
This doesn't have to be physical.
Your mouth is a deadly weapon!
REPENT, LORD FORGIVE US!

Comments and Notes:

Day 162

NUGGETS OF TRUTH

A heart that devises wicked plans, Feet that are swift in running to evil, A false witness who speaks lies. And one who sows discord among brethren.

PROVERBS 6:18-19

One must stop plotting and scheming evil plots, Gossiping and causing disagreements between Church, acquaintances, family or people in general. God is not pleased!

Comments and Notes:

_____

_____

_____

_____

Day 163

NUGGETS OF TRUTH

My son, keep your father's command, and do not forsake the law of your mother.

PROVERBS 6:20

Regardless of our age
Our parents should be honored and obeyed.
This will ensure longevity for us.

Comments and Notes:

Day 164

NUGGETS OF TRUTH

Say to wisdom, "You are my sister," And call understanding your nearest kin.

PROVERBS 7:4

**Wisdom is liken to two sisters,
They will defend each other
While understanding is ones closest relative.
Will you be there for each other?**

Comments and Notes:

_____

_____

_____

_____

_____

Day 165

NUGGETS OF TRUTH

All the words of my mouth are With righteousness; Nothing crooked or perverse is in them.

PROVERBS 8:8

The words we speak must be
The very WORDS of God.
In Him there's no corruption!

Comments and Notes:

___
___
___
___

Day 166

NUGGETS OF TRUTH

*Does not wisdom cry out,
And understanding lift up her voice?*

PROVERBS 8:1

Godly and supreme Wisdom
Has a voice that shouts
Boldly and echoes loud.
Can you hear her voice?

Comments and Notes:

Day 167

NUGGETS OF TRUTH

Listen, for I will speak of excellent things, and from the opening of my lips will come right things.

PROVERBS 8:6

**Pay close attention to the announcement
And sayings of GOD'S word
For they are our life!**

Comments and Notes:

_____

_____

_____

_____

_____

Day 168

NUGGETS OF TRUTH

Receive my instruction, and not silver, and knowledge rather than choice gold; For wisdom is better than rubies, and all the things one may desire cannot be compared with her.

PROVERBS 8:10 – 11

Our heavenly Father's instructions,
Directions and revelations
Surpasses any precious metals, jewels,
Diamonds, stones even limitless revenue
There's no comparison at all!

Comments and Notes:

_____

_____

Day 169

NUGGETS OF TRUTH

*I, wisdom, dwell with prudence,
And find out knowledge
And discretion.*

PROVERBS 8:12

Wisdom and knowledge brings
Practical insight to manage the
Affairs of life by not disclosing Godly truths.
Some matters are between you and God alone!

Comments and Notes:

Day 170

NUGGETS OF TRUTH

The LORD possessed me at the Beginning of His way, Before His works of old.

PROVERBS 8:22

**WISDOM is God's possession
In the beginning of creation
After six days of completion then rest
Now and throughout eternity.**

Comments and Notes:

_____

_____

_____

_____

_____

_____

Day 171

NUGGETS OF TRUTH

I have been established from everlasting, from the beginning, before there was ever an earth.

PROVERBS 8:23

**The foundation of God
Is His insurmountable wisdom.**

Comments and Notes:

_____

_____

_____

_____

_____

_____

_____

Day 172

NUGGETS OF TRUTH

Now therefore, listen to me, my children,
For blessed are those who keep My ways.

PROVERBS 8:32

Pay attention, and obey the
Voice of God's word.
He's always speaking, can you hear Him?

Comments and Notes:

Day 173

NUGGETS OF TRUTH

And Phillip said, If you believe with all your heart That Jesus is the Messiah and accept Him as the Author of your salvation In the kingdom of God, Giving Him your obedience, then You may. And he replied, I do believe That Jesus is the Christ is the Son of God.

ACTS 8:37 -AMP

One must believe on the Lord Jesus Just as Phillip did. Jesus is the Anointed Messiah; Accept Him as your Author of Salvation; Denounce Satan as lord; Abhor evil cling to what is good. You are now saved to the glory of God!
The heavenly hosts of angels are rejoicing!

Comments and Notes:

Day 174

NUGGETS OF TRUTH

*Hear instruction and be wise,
And do not disdain it.*

PROVERBS 8:33

Listening to and obeying the word of the Lord brings wisdom.

Comments and Notes:

Day 175

NUGGETS OF TRUTH

Blessed is the man,
who listens to me,
Watching daily at my gates,
Waiting at the posts of my doors.

PROVERBS 8:34

One will receive spiritual blessings
By following and adhering to Godly counsel and
guarding the entrance of your gates.

Comments and Notes:

Day 176

NUGGETS OF TRUTH

For whoever finds me finds life.
And obtains favor from the LORD;
But those who sins against me
Wrongs his own soul;
All those who hate me love death.

PROVERBS 8:35-36

Spiritual life begins after the new birth;
Then God's favor shows up;
But willful sin leads only to destruction.

Comments and Notes:

_____

_____

_____

_____

Day 177

NUGGETS OF TRUTH

I am the vine you are the branches.
He who abides in me, and I in him,
Bears much fruit;
for without me
You can do nothing.

JOHN 15:5

Our lives will flourish as we are being
Nourished from Jesus Christ;
When maturity is reached more fruit
Is reproduced. For with God
all things are possible.

Comments and Notes:

_____

_____

_____

Day 178

NUGGETS OF TRUTH

If you live in Me (abide vitally united to Me) and My words remain in you and continue to live in your hearts, asks whatever you will, and it Shall be done for you.

JOHN 15:7 -AMP

While we live by the word daily;
Allowing it to transform us
The Lord will give us the desires of our heart.
Lord teach us every day to depend on You!

Comments and Notes:

_____

_____

_____

_____

Day 179

NUGGETS OF TRUTH

I will do (I Myself will grant) whatever you ask in My Name (as presenting all that IAM), so that the Father may be glorified and extolled in (through) the Son.

JOHN 14:13 -AMP

One must permit the Greater One
To be a Blessing to us, so the Father
Will be magnified in the Son.
How do you glorify the Father daily?

Comments and Notes:

Day 180

NUGGETS OF TRUTH

Yes I will grant (I Myself will do for you) whatever you ask in My Name (As presenting all that I AM).

JOHN 14:14 - AMP

Let's face it being obedient to the
Lord will cause our prayers to be answered.
Are your prayers being answered;
On your own merit or someone else's?

Comments and Notes:

Day 181

NUGGETS OF TRUTH

If you (really) love Me, you will keep (obey) My commands.

JOHN 14:15 - AMP

Love causes a person to submit,
Trust, acknowledge and obey instructions
From the Lord even when he doesn't
Have all the insight.

Comments and Notes:

Day 182

NUGGETS OF TRUTH

And I will ask the Father, and He will give You another Comforter (Counselor, Helper, Intercessor, Advocate, Strengthener, And standby) that He may remain with you forever.

JOHN 14:16 - AMP

God prayed for us so that we would
Not be left alone; the Comforter has attributes
To help aid us in all areas of our lives.
Will you accept His assistance?

Comments and Notes:

_____

_____

Day 183

NUGGETS OF TRUTH

The Spirit of Truth, whom the world cannot receive (welcome, take to its heart), because it does not see Him or know and recognize Him, for He lives with you (constantly) and will be in you.

JOHN 14:17 - AMP

Persons that have not received or
Are not filled with the Holy Spirit can't recognize
Him without the Holy Spirit residing in them!
Selah!

Comments and Notes:

Day 184

NUGGETS OF TRUTH

Jesus answered and said unto him, If a man love me, he will keep my words: And my Father will love him, and we will come unto him, And make our abode with him.

JOHN 14:23

Having love for the Lord will compel a person to be submitted, obedient, dedicated to God's word then Jesus will live inside of you.

Comments and Notes:

_____

_____

_____

_____

Day 185

NUGGETS OF TRUTH

But the Comforter the Holy Spirit, Whom the Father will send in My Name (in My place, to represent Me and act on behalf), He will teach You all things, and He will cause You to recall everything I told you.

JOHN 14:26 AMP

The Blessed Holy Spirit with His benefit plan Is available for the believer which comes from the Father to represent Him; He will recall and bring things back to our Remembrance that has been deposited in us!

Comments and Notes:

_____

_____

Day 186

NUGGETS OF TRUTH

Do Not let your heart be troubled (distressed, agitated), You believe in And adhere to and trust in and rely on God; Believe in and adhere to and trust in and rely also on Me.

JOHN 14:1 - AMP

Avoid heartaches, distressed, oppression And being aggravated. Now, one must Confidently trust and rely on God. He is faithful!

Comments and Notes:

_____

_____

_____

_____

Day 187

NUGGETS OF TRUTH

Jesus said to him, I am the Way And the Truth and the Life; No one comes to the Father Except by (through) Me.

JOHN 14:6 - AMP

There is no other way to get to God,
Unless one goes through Jesus Christ!
One can learn more in the sixty-six books!

Comments and Notes:

Day 188

NUGGETS OF TRUTH

**If you acknowledge and confess
With your lips that Jesus is Lord
and in your heart believe
That God raised Him from the dead,
You will be saved.**

ROMANS 10:9-10-AMP

When you repent, pray and ask the Lord to forgive you, believe in your heart that God raised Jesus from the dead you shall be saved.
This is an act of confession of faith!

Comments and Notes:

_____

_____

_____

_____

Day 189

NUGGETS OF TRUTH

God is a Spirit; and they that worship him
Must worship him in spirit
And in truth.

JOHN 4:24

A person must worship God
In the Spirit because He is a Spirit.
His word is truth and reveals who we are in Him!

Comments and Notes:

Day 190

NUGGETS OF TRUTH

Jesus answered him, I assure you, most solemnly I tell you, that unless a person is born again (anew, from above), he cannot ever see (know, be acquainted with, and experience) the Kingdom of God.

JOHN 3:3 - AMP

If you desire to go to heaven
Then you must repent, ask for forgiveness,
Receive Jesus as Lord and Savior,
Live a Holy life for the Lord;
In order to inherit eternal life!
Oh by the way, let's extend this invitation to others!

Comments and Notes:

_____

_____

Day 191

NUGGETS OF TRUTH

Nicodemus said to Him, How a man can be born when he is old? Can he enter his mother's womb again and be born?

JOHN 3:4 - AMP

The new birth is available to any gender.
Male or female can experience this life changing event.
This is not a natural birth!
It is Spiritual!

Comments and Notes:

_____

_____

Day 192

NUGGETS OF TRUTH

Jesus answered, I assure, most solemnly I tell you, unless man is born of water and (even) the Spirit, he cannot (ever) enter The kingdom of God.

JOHN 3:5 - AMP

The Messiah (Jesus Christ) assures us that
The new birth is spiritual and available in order to gain the keys to the kingdom!
Will your key fit any door in glory?

Comments and Notes:

_____

_____

_____

_____

Day 193

NUGGETS OF TRUTH

What is born of and (from) the flesh is flesh (of the physical is physical); And what is born of the Spirit is spirit.

JOHN 3:6

The natural birth is vital in order to reside on this earth; However, a spiritual birth is vital in order to live in heaven!

Comments and Notes:

Day 194

NUGGETS OF TRUTH

*Lay not up for yourselves treasures upon Earth, where moth and rust doth corrupt, and where thieves break through and steal;
But lay up for yourselves treasures in heaven, where thieves do not break through nor steal*

MATTHEW 6:19-20

Our focus and concerned should be
Heavenly bound where it is free from
Destruction, decay, tarnish metals
No thieves or burglary allowed!

Comments and Notes:

_____

_____

Day 195

NUGGETS OF TRUTH

For where your treasure is, there will your heart may be also.

MATTHEW 6:21

One's heart must exhibit heavenly riches,
Material possessions will be dissolved.

Comments and Notes:

Day 196

NUGGETS OF TRUTH

No man can serve two masters; for either he will hate the one, and love the other; or he will stand by and be devoted to the one and despise and be against the other. You cannot serve God and mammon (Deceitful riches, money, possessions, or whatever is trusted in).

MATTHEW 6:24 - AMP

Decide who will have authority or rule over you; Chose the Lord or Satan not both at the same time. Where will your allegiance be?

Comments and Notes:

Day 197

NUGGETS OF TRUTH

Therefore I tell you, stop being perpetually uneasy (anxious and worried) about your life, what you shall eat or what you shall drink; Or about your body, what you shall put on is not life greater (in quality) than food, and the body (far above and more excellent) than clothing?

MATTHEW 6:25 - AMP

Trust in the Lord for He knows our daily needs. One's life is more valuable than materials processions.

Comments and Notes:

Day 198

NUGGETS OF TRUTH

Blessed (happy to be envied and spiritually prosperous — with life-joy and satisfaction in God's favor and salvation; Regardless of their outward conditions) are the poor in spirit (the humble, who rate themselves Insignificant), for theirs Is the kingdom of heaven!

MATTHEW 5:3 -AMP

It is possible for us to live a blessed,
Prosperous life and rest in God's favor
Regardless of our lot in life.
Staying humble brings kingdom blessings.

Comments and Notes:

Day 199

NUGGETS OF TRUTH

Blessed and enviable happy (with a happiness produced by the experience of God's favor
And especially conditioned by the revelation of His matchless grace)
Are those who mourn, for they shall be comforted!

MATTHEW 5:4 - AMP

God will anoint and comfort His people
That mourns as they experience
His compassion, mercy, happiness and favor!

Comments and Notes:

_____

_____

Day 200

NUGGETS OF TRUTH

*Blessed (happy, blithesome, joyous,
Spiritually prosperous — with life-joy
And satisfaction in God's favor
And salvation, regardless of their
Outward conditions) are the meek
(The mild patient, longsuffering),
For they shall inherit the earth!*

MATTHEW 5:5 - AMP

The meek are joyous, spiritually prosperous,
With life, joy and God's favor.

Comment and Notes:

_____

_____

_____

Day 201

NUGGETS OF TRUTH

Blessed and fortunate and happy and spiritually prosperous (in the state in which the born-again child of God enjoys His favor salvation) are those who hunger and thirst for righteousness (uprightness and right standing with God), for they shall be completely satisfied!

MATTHEW 5:6 - AMP

Those that are born again
Have the privilege of prospering
Because of being in covenant with
God and complete satisfaction is guaranteed.

Comments and Notes:

Day 202

NUGGETS OF TRUTH

Then Jesus was led (guided) by the Holy Spirit into the wilderness (desert) to be tempted (tested and tried) by the devil.

MATTHEW 4:1 - AMP

The anointing from the Lord will give us victory as our tests are being administered. Be careful during your test; time for an attitude check!

Comments and Notes:

Day 203

Nuggets of Truth

And he went without food for forty days and forty nights, and later He was hungry. And the tempter came and said to Him, If you are God's Son, command these stones to be made (loaves of) bread.

Matthew 4: 2-3 - Amp

Fasting will cause our spirit man to Become sensitive in Spiritual battles. The lord's word is the bread of Life. Do you want a slice or the whole loaf?

Comments and Notes:

_____

_____

_____

Day 204

NUGGETS OF TRUTH

But He replied, It has been written, Man Shall not live and be upheld and sustained by Bread alone, but by every word that comes forth from the mouth of God.

MATTHEW 4:4 -AMP

God's word is our daily bread;
One must eat, meditate declare and decree
The word as it is coming from God's lips.
Whose words are coming out of your mouth?

Comments and Notes:

_____

_____

_____

Day 205

NUGGETS OF TRUTH

Then the devil took Him into the holy city and placed Him on a turret (pinnacle, gable) of the temple sanctuary. And said to Him, If you are the Son of God, throw yourself down; for it is written, He will give His angels charge over you, and they will bear you up on their hands, lest you strike your foot against a stone.

MATTHEW 4: 5-6 - AMP

Don't allow the devil to tempt or entice you
By offering the world.
It doesn't belong to him.
If one compromise, his soul can be lost.

Comments and Notes:

Day 206

NUGGETS OF TRUTH

Jesus said unto him, It is written again, Thou shall not temp the Lord thou God. Again, then the devil took Him up on a very high mountain and showed Him all the kingdoms of the world and the glory (the splendor, Magnificence, preeminence, And excellence of them.

MATTHEW 4: 7-8 - AMP

When the devil comes to tempt us
One must speak God's word.
Oppose the devil and he will flee!

Comments and Notes:

Day 207

NUGGETS OF TRUTH

And he said to Him, these things all taken together; I will give You, if You Will prostrate Yourself before me and do homage and worship me.

MATTHEW 4: 9 - AMP

The devil desires to steal our worship from God.
But one must not give him any place!
Put up a sign: No trespassing – private property!

Comments and Notes:

Day 208

NUGGETS OF TRUTH

Then Jesus said to him, Begone, Satan! It has been written, You shall worship the Lord your God, and Him Alone shall you serve.

MATTHEW 4:10 - AMP

Speak to Satan and convey: Be gaged!
In the name of Jesus!
Declare and decree your allegiance to God alone.
Abba Father deserves our whole heart worship!

Comments and Notes:

Day 209

NUGGETS OF TRUTH

Then the devil departed from Him, And behold the angels came and Ministered to Him.

MATTHEW 4: 11- AMP

After being tested the Holy Spirit
Will minister, encourage and strengthen
Us as well. The Lord allows us to be tested at times.
Will you pass or fail?

Comments and Notes:

_____

_____

_____

_____

_____

Day 210

NUGGETS OF TRUTH

Let your light so shine before men,
That they may see your good works,
And glorify your Father
Which is in heaven.

MATTHEW 5:16

God is glorified in heaven as one
Allows their light to shine.
Will you live a Holy life on purpose? Selah!!
Your light will cause sin to take flight!

Comments and Notes:

_____

_____

_____

_____

_____

Day 211

NUGGETS OF TRUTH

Think not that I am come to destroy the law or the prophets: I am not come to destroy but to fulfil.

MATTHEW 5:17

Jesus fulfilled the law by coming
To this earth to redeem mankind.
Have you been redeemed or are you
Still playing church?

Comments and Notes:

Day 212

NUGGETS OF TRUTH

But I say unto you, whosoever Is angry with his brother without A cause shall be in danger of judgment; and whosoever shall to his brother, Raca, shall be in danger of the council: But whosoever shall say, Thou fool, shall be in danger Of hell fire.

MATTHEW 5:22

It is a serious matter being angry
With our sisters or brothers without cause.
Avoid character assassination with your words.
The tongue can cause an annihilation of a forest!

Comments and Notes:

Day 213

NUGGETS OF TRUTH

Therefore if thou bring thy gift to the altar, and there remember that thy brother hath ought against thee.

MATTHEW 5:23

A person needs to be free from
Any hidden form of unforgiveness.
Get it right. The Holy Spirit is watching!

Comments and Notes:

Day 214

NUGGETS OF TRUTH

Leave your gift at the altar, And go. First make peace with your brother, and then come back and present your gift.

MATTHEW 5:24 - AMP

Put you tithes and or offering on the alter
Seek out your brother, ask for forgiveness
In humility, then present your gift to God.
One's attitude matters to the Lord!
It is a matter of the Heart!

Comments and Notes:

_____

_____

_____

_____

Day 215

NUGGETS OF TRUTH

Therefore be imitators of God (copy Him and follow His example), as well-beloved children (imitate their father).

EPHESIANS 5:1 - AMP

Jesus Christ is our role model;
He's the ultimate example
Of love, mercy, grace and compassion.

Comments and Notes:

Day 216

NUGGETS OF TRUTH

And walk in love, (esteeming and delighting in one another) as Christ loved us and gave Himself up for us, slain offering and sacrifice to God (for you, so that it became) a sweet fragrance.

EPHESIANS 5:2 - AMP

Go after love continually, just like Jesus Christ
He loved and gifted Himself for us
Because of His sacrifice this gives
Off a pleasant fragrance to God!
Praise the name of the Lord!

Comments and Notes:

Day 217

NUGGETS OF TRUTH

May blessing (praise, laudation, and eulogy) be to the God and Father of our Lord Jesus Christ (the Messiah) Who has blessed us in Christ with every spiritual (given by the Holy Spirit) blessing in the heavenly realm!

EPHESIANS 1:3 - AMP

Lift up you voice on purpose
By blessing our God and Father
Through the anointed one Jesus Christ.

Comments and Notes:

Day 218

NUGGETS OF TRUTH

And the scripture, foreseeing that God would justify (declare righteous, put in right standing with Himself) the Gentiles in consequence of faith, proclaimed the Gospel to Abraham in the promise, saying, In you shall the nations (of the earth) be blessed.

GALATIANS 3: 8 - AMP

When a person receives the Gospel of Jesus Christ one is justified, declared righteous, it puts (the gentiles in right standing with God. It is because of Him all the Nations can receive these blessings.

Comments and Notes:

Day 219

Nuggets of Truth

Christ hath redeemed us from the curse of the law, being made a curse for us; for it is written,
Cursed is every one that hangs on a tree.

Galatians 3:13

Before salvation we were sin sick souls.
Jesus brought us back paid the penalty
Of sin with the shedding of His blood.
He went to the cross and became a curse for us.
Living a Holy life and sharing Christ with
Others will cause heaven to rejoice over new souls.

Comments and Notes:

Day 220

NUGGETS OF TRUTH

That the blessings of Abraham might come on the Gentiles through Jesus Christ; that we might receive the promise of the Spirit through faith.

GALATIANS 3:14

Abraham blessings can be ours
Because of the second Adam Jesus Christ's
Sacrificial death for the world.
Have you received any Promises yet?

Comments and Notes:

Day 221

NUGGETS OF TRUTH

So, then, those who are people of faith are blessed and made happy and favored by God (as Partners in fellowship) with the believing and trusting Abraham.

GALATIANS 3:9 - AMP

After a person receives Jesus Christ
As Savior by Faith one comes
Into a covenant relationship as Abraham Seed.
Are you a son of flesh or son of the promise?

Comments and Notes:

Day 222

NUGGETS OF TRUTH

Now What I mean is that as long as the inferior (heir) is a child and under age, he does not differ from a slave, although he is the master of all the estate.

GALATIANS 4:1 - AMP

Before an heir receives his inheritance
He should become mature, obtain
Skillful and wise counsel from elders;
Also have financial guidance.

Comments and Notes:

_____

_____

_____

_____

Day 223

Nuggets of Truth

But he is under guardians and administrators or trustees until the date fixed by his father.

Galatians 4:2 - Amp

A young person inheritance can be in
A trust fund, legal guardians or
An appointee until he is sound minded
And mature to handle his finances.
Why do you want to rush the process?
Wait for your net worth!

Comments and Notes:

_____

_____

_____

_____

Day 224

NUGGETS OF TRUTH

So we (Jewish Christians) also, when we were minors, were kept like slaves under (the rules of the Hebrew ritual and subject to) the elementary teachings of a system of external observations and regulations.

GALATIANS 4:3 - AMP

Being a spiritual Jew entitles
A person to all the benefits of kingdom heirs.

Comments and Notes:

_____

_____

_____

_____

Day 225

NUGGETS OF TRUTH

But when the proper time had fully come, God sent His Son, born of a woman, born subject to (the regulations of) the Law.

GALATIANS 4:4 - AMP

Jesus was born into the world to save us from our sins. His parental parents were not exempt from any laws.

Comments and Notes:

_____

_____

_____

_____

_____

Day 226

NUGGETS OF TRUTH

To redeem them that were under the law, that we might receive the adoption of sons.

GALATIANS 4:5

Jesus purchased us from slavery (redeemed) from sin. We have been adopted as sons of God,
So one is no longer under the law.
Thank you Jesus for your Blood!

Comments and Notes:

_____

_____

_____

_____

_____

Day 227

NUGGETS OF TRUTH

And because you (really) are (His) sons, God has sent the (Holy) Spirit of His Son into our hearts, crying, ABBA (Father) Father!

GALATIANS 4:6 - AMP

The expression "ABBA FATHER" is
Exclusively for Sons of God.
Being led by the Holy Spirit one cries out
From the depths of our hearts.
Let me hear you call HIM!

Comments and Notes:

_____

_____

_____

_____

Day 228

NUGGETS OF TRUTH

In this freedom Christ has made us free (and completely liberated us); Stand fast then and do not hampered and held Ensnared and submit again to a yoke of slavery (which you have once put off).

GALATIANS 5:1 - AMP

Because one is no longer bound by the law Jesus Christ's Blood liberated us.
So, a person should no longer be enslaved by willful sin.

Comments and Notes:

_____

_____

Day 229

NUGGETS OF TRUTH

If you seek to be justified and declared righteous and to be given a right standing with God through the Law, you are brought to nothing And so separated (severed) from Christ. You have fallen away from grace (from God's gracious favor and unmerited blessing).

GALATIANS 5: 4 - AMP

A person is declared right by the Blood of the Lamb, this is available Through the grace and favor of God.

Comments and Notes:

Day 230

NUGGETS OF TRUTH

For (if we are) in Christ Jesus, neither circumcision nor uncircumcision counts for Anything, but only faith activated And energized and expressed And working through love.

GALATIANS 5:6 - AMP

Jesus Christ is not concerned about our gender. He moves by our obedience, love and faith Being operative and being confident in Him Now manifestations are visible.

Comments and Notes:

Day 231

NUGGETS OF TRUTH

A little leaven leaveneth the whole lump.

GALATIANS 5:9

Leaven is an ingredient used in yeast
To make dough rise.
Sin is like decay in a tooth, if not removed
It can destroy a perfectly good tooth.
Willful and not repenting of sin leads to death!

Comments and Notes:

Day 232

NUGGETS OF TRUTH

You were running the race nobly. Who has interfered in (hindered and stopped you from) Your heeding and following the Truth?

GALATIANS 5:7 - AMP

During this journey of life
Do not allow anyone to interfere
With the progress of your Spiritual growth.
Don't worry about the other runners, run your race!
Selah!

Comments and Notes:

_____

_____

_____

Day 233

NUGGETS OF TRUTH

This (evil) persuasion is not from Him who called you (who invited you to freedom in Christ).

GALATIANS 5:8 - AMP

The devil is behind all deception.
One must recognize his tactics and Strategies.
Liberty comes from Jesus!

Comments and Notes:

Day 234

NUGGETS OF TRUTH

Look out for those dogs (Judaizers, legalists), Look out for those mischief-makers, Look out for those who mutilate the flesh.

PHILIPPIANS 3:2 - AMP

Paul taught the necessity of circumcision,
But in reality it is a ritual without
The correct heart condition.

Comments and Notes:

Day 235

NUGGETS OF TRUTH

For we (Christians) are the true circumcision, who worship God in spirit and by the Spirit of God and exult and glory and pride ourselves in Jesus Christ and put no confidence or dependence in the flesh and outward privileges and physical advantages and external appearances.

PHILIPPIANS 3:3 - AMP

There is no profit or gain in our flesh. We are part body, soul, spirit; mind will and emotions. With the baptism of the Holy Spirit one can overcome the world because the greater one lives in us!

Comments and Notes:

Day 236

NUGGETS OF TRUTH

But what things were gained to me, Those I counted loss for Christ.

PHILIPPIANS 3:7

Prestige, accolades or educational achievements Doesn't compare to God's Favor or grace on our lives! The sacrifice of Christ outweighs any accomplishments!

Comments and Notes:

_____

_____

_____

_____

_____

_____

_____

Day 237

NUGGETS OF TRUTH

Not as though I had already attained, either were already perfect: But I follow after, if that I May apprehend that for which also I am apprehended of Christ Jesus.

PHILIPPIANS 3:12

No achievement in this life can compare
To a person that is seeking the Lord,
Devoting themselves in prayer
And intimate worship!

Comments and Notes:

Day 238

NUGGETS OF TRUTH

*Brethren, I count not myself
to have apprehended:
But this one thing I do,
Forgetting those things
which are behind,
And reaching forth unto
Those things which are before.*

PHILIPPIANS 3:13

It is imperative that one let go of past hurts,
Then stretch towards the heavenly calling.
Earnestly pursue after Him!

Comments and Notes:

_____

_____

Day 239

Nuggets of Truth

I press on toward the goal to win the (Supreme and heavenly) prize to which God in Christ Jesus is calling upward.

Philippians 3:14 - AMP

Our goal every day is for God's approval.
He has promised to give us a crown of life.
Look up your redemption is near.

Comments and Notes:

Day 240

NUGGETS OF TRUTH

So let those (of us) who are spiritually mature and full-grown have this mind and hold these convictions; and if any Respect you have a different attitude of mind, God will make that clear to you also.

PHILIPPIANS 3:15 - AMP

The Lord will reveal His plans to
Mature adults the ones that listen
And obey quickly, in order to receive
Instructions regarding the upward call.

Comments and Notes:

_____

_____

Day 241

Nuggets of Truth

Only let us hold true to what we have already attained and walk and order our lives by that.

Philippians 3:16 - Amp

One should not allow anyone
Or circumstances to change
Our Christianity or Godly devotion!
Our allegiance is to God.

Comments and Notes:

Day 242

NUGGETS OF TRUTH

Rejoice in the Lord always (delight, gladden Yourselves in Him); Again I say rejoice!

PHILIPPIANS 4:4 - AMP

**To know the Lord, and being
In constant fellowship with Him
Causes exuberant rejoicing.
Inhale and Exhale rejoice evermore!**

Comments and Notes:

Day 243

NUGGETS OF TRUTH

Let all men know and perceive and recognize your unselfishness your (your considerate and forebearing spirit). The Lord is near (He is coming soon).

PHILIPPIANS 4:5 - AMP

As a person acknowledge and live
A Holy Life in private or public
This portrays the Love of God.
One realizes that He is on His way Back soon!

Comments and Notes:

_____

_____

_____

_____

Day 244

NUGGETS OF TRUTH

Do not fret or have any anxiety about anything, but in circumstance and in Everything, by prayer and petition (Definite requests), with thanksgiving, continue to make your wants known To God.

PHILIPPIANS 4:6 - AMP

Living a life of prayer is an antidote
For dread, fear, or any anxiety
That tries to enter our mind.
Prayer and Faith gives us access to the kingdom!

Comments and Notes:

_____

_____

_____

Day 245

NUGGETS OF TRUTH

And the God's peace which transcends all Understanding shall garrison and Mount guard over your hearts And minds in Christ Jesus.

PHILIPPIANS 4:7 - AMP

The peace that we receive
From the Lord is perfect.
Shalom is Hebrew for Peace!
God's peace makes us whole lacking nothing!
Have you experienced this Peace?

Comments and Notes:

_____

_____

_____

Day 246

NUGGETS OF TRUTH

*The Lord your God will bless you
In all your works and in all
To which you put your hand.*

DEUTERONOMY 15:10b

Here is another promise
From our Father to bless our
Hands from honest labor.
Are your hands blessed or cursed?

Comments and Notes:

_____

_____

_____

_____

_____

Day 247

NUGGETS OF TRUTH

The Spirit of a man will sustain him In sickness, but who can bear a broken spirit?

PROVERBS 18:14

Even when we are ill and sickness
Attacks our bodies – it is at this time
That our spirit can support, encourage, aid,
Nourish and heal us back to a healthy state.
Jesus our High Priest took our sickness!

Comments and Notes:

Day 248

NUGGETS OF TRUTH

Always in every prayer of mine making request for you all with joy.

PHILIPPIANS 1:4

It is expedient that you are aware that someone is interceding in prayer on your behalf.
The Holy Spirit makes intercessions for us!
We need to covet these prayers!

Comments and Notes:

Day 249

NUGGETS OF TRUTH

The name of the Lord is a strong tower; The righteous run to it and are safe.

PROVERBS 18:10

In Jesus name there is safety, run into
That name (JESUS) strength resides in Him!
Lord we desire your strength NOW!

Comments and Notes:

Day 250

NUGGETS OF TRUTH

A brother offended is harder to win Than a strong city And contention are like the bars of a castle.

PROVERBS 18:19

One must be careful when speaking,
Words can build up or destroy
Ask him to forgive you;
Restoration is sure to follow!

Comments and Notes:

Day 251

NUGGETS OF TRUTH

And He Himself gave some to be Apostles, some prophets, some evangelist And some pastors and teachers.

EPHESIANS 4:11

Despite contrary beliefs
The five-fold Hand Ministry
Is still operative in the body of Christ.
Are the gifts manifested in your local Church?

Comments and Notes:

Day 252

NUGGETS OF TRUTH

He who has knowledge spares his words, And a man of understanding is of a calm spirit.

PROVERBS 17:27

Where there is Skillful and Godly wisdom Words will be limited resulting in peace! Selah! (Pause calmly and think about this.)

Comments and Notes:

_____

_____

_____

_____

_____

Day 253

NUGGETS OF TRUTH

For John truly baptized with water, But you shall be baptized with the Holy Spirit not many days from now.

ACTS 1:5

The HOLY SPIRIT Baptism
Is available for anyone after salvation!
Have you been filled with the Holy Spirit?
What is the evidence?

Comments and Notes:

Day 254

NUGGETS OF TRUTH

Therefore, when they had come together, they asked Him, saying, "Lord, will You at this time restore the kingdom to Israel?"

ACTS 1:6

Pray this prayer:
Thy kingdom come,
Your will be done on earth today!

Comments and Notes:

_____

_____

_____

_____

_____

Day 255

NUGGETS OF TRUTH

And He said to them, "It is not for you to know times or seasons which the Father has put in His own authority."

ACTS 1:7

One should not be overly consumed
With the time for the return of Jesus.
However, living a Holy life is necessary.
Grateful expectancy is a vital necessity.
Are you ready?

Comments and Notes:

_____

_____

_____

_____

Day 256

NUGGETS OF TRUTH

But you shall receive power when the Holy Spirit has come upon you; And you shall be witnesses To Me in Jerusalem, and in all Judea and Samaria, and to the end of the earth.

ACTS 1:8

The HOLY SPIRIT releases *dunamis*.
Why? It is for the Glory of God.
Stop taking credit for what's not yours!
Lord help our selfish motives!!!

Comments and Notes:

Day 257

Nuggets of Truth

Now when He had spoken these things, while they watched, He was taken up and a cloud received Him out of their sight.

Acts 1:9

Jesus was taken into heaven
My question for you is:
Will you receive a heavenly escort?
Selah

Comments and Notes:

Day 258

NUGGETS OF TRUTH

But a certain man named Ananias with Sapphira his wife, sold a possession.

ACTS 5:1

Be careful when disclosing a vow to the Lord. You will reap what you sow!

Comments and Notes:

Day 259

Nuggets of Truth

And he kept part of the proceeds, His wife also being aware of it, and brought a Certain part and laid it at the apostles feet.

Acts 5:2

Give the whole tenth of your tithe not part.
Don't allow anyone to cause you to sin;
Not even your spouse. God is too Holy!

Comments and Notes:

Day 260

NUGGETS OF TRUTH

But Peter said, "Ananias, why has Satan filled your heart to lie to the Holy Spirit and keep back part of the price of the land for yourself?"

ACTS 5:3

When a person lies in general,
They are lying to the Holy Spirit!
Sin crouches at the door!

Comments and Notes:

Day 261

NUGGETS OF TRUTH

While it remained, was it not your own? And after it was sold, was it not in your own control? Why have you conceived This thing in your heart? You have not lied To men but to God.

ACTS 5:4

Do not cause your flesh to sin
By speaking deceit and having lying lips.
Both are an abomination to the Lord!!!

Comments and Notes:

_____

_____

Day 262

NUGGETS OF TRUTH

Then the twelve summoned the multitude of the disciples and said, Is it not desirable that we should Leave the word of God and serve tables.

ACTS 6:2

It is fitting for Pastors, Ministers
And or leaders to delegate
Or commission others for kingdom work.
Living a Holy life and being a tither is imperative.
Are you qualified to be THE CALLED?

Comments and Notes:

_____

_____

_____

Day 263

NUGGETS OF TRUTH

Therefore brethren seek out from among you seven men of good reputation, full of the Holy Spirit and wisdom, whom We may appoint over this business;

ACTS 6:3

Persons in leadership position
Must watch, pray and seek the face
Of the Lord in order to select Holy Ghost
Persons male or female for God's House!
Are you man led or Spirit led?

Comments and Notes:

_____

_____

_____

Day 264

NUGGETS OF TRUTH

But we will give ourselves continually To prayer and to the ministry Of the word.

ACTS 6:4

Spending time in pray and studying
The word is our life supply.
Without natural food a person may die.
Likewise, without the Holy Word which is God,
One may become spiritually dead!
Who partakes of the most food flesh or spirit?

Comments and Notes:

_____

_____

_____

_____

_____

Day 265

NUGGETS OF TRUTH

And the saying pleased the whole Multitude. And they chose Stephen, A man full of faith and the Holy Spirit.

ACTS 6:5

When a person speaks the word of the Lord
His Word is Anointed to remove
Burdens and destroy yolks.
Are you speaking faith filled words?

Comments and Notes:

Day 266

NUGGETS OF TRUTH

And he said, "Get out of your country and from your relatives and come to a land that I will show you."

ACTS 7:3

Sometimes one may have to leave his family
Surrender all to follow and
Receive the divine blessing from God.
How far will you go to receive God's Favor?

Comments and Notes:

_____

_____

_____

_____

_____

Day 267

NUGGETS OF TRUTH

And God gave him no inheritance in it not even enough to set his foot on. But even when Abraham had no child, He promised to give it to him for a possession, and to his Descendants after him.

ACTS 7:5

The father of Faith didn't have any children,
But held on the promises of God's word
That was spoken to him by God Himself.
The word of God will speak and perform!

Comments and Notes:

Day 268

NUGGETS OF TRUTH

On the same day, when evening had come, He said to them, "Let us cross over to the other side."

MARK 4:35

Avoid being so stationary because your blessings maybe in another geographic
Location waiting for that divine appointment.

Comments and Notes:

_____

_____

_____

_____

_____

Day 269

NUGGETS OF TRUTH

And a great windstorm arose, and the waves beat into the boat, So that it was already filling.

MARK 4:37

Stay in faith even in the
Mist of storms, disappointments
Lack or calamity.
Our God Supersedes all of these!

Comments and Notes:

Day 270

NUGGETS OF TRUTH

But He was in the stern, asleep on a pillow. And they awoke Him and said to Him, "Teacher, do You care that we are perishing?"

MARK 4:38

The Lord is aware of our life issues.
He will not permit them to overwhelm us.
Do you trust God in spite of negative appearances?

Comments and Notes:

_____

_____

_____

_____

_____

Day 271

NUGGETS OF TRUTH

Then He arose and rebuked the wind, and said to the sea, Peace be still! And the wind ceased and there Was a great calm.

MARK 4:39

When the Lord speaks His words
Are anointed and can change our life.
One rhema word from Him alters our destiny
While giving us His PEACE!

Comments and Notes:

_____

_____

_____

_____

_____

Day 272

NUGGETS OF TRUTH

But He said to them, "Why are you so Fearful? How is it that you Have no faith?"

MARK 4:40

Faith and fear can't exist at the same time.
Which one do you possess, faith or fear?
Faith is spiritual but fear is of the sin nature.

Comments and Notes:

Day 273

NUGGETS OF TRUTH

*If anyone has ears to hear,
Let him hear.*

MARK 4:23

The HOLY SPIRIT Is always speaking.
Listening and hearing are different!
Can you hear His voice?

Comments and Notes:

_____

_____

_____

_____

_____

_____

Day 274

NUGGETS OF TRUTH

The glory of this latter temple shall be greater that the former, says the Lord of hosts. And in this place I will give peace, Says the Lord of hosts.

HAGGAI 2:9

All of us should have a secret closet.
This place is where the glory
Of the Lord will invade and rest on us.
His desire is to dine with His children.

Comments and Notes:

_____

_____

_____

_____

Day 275

NUGGETS OF TRUTH

For thus says the Lord of hosts: He sent Me after, glory, to the nations which plunder you; for he who touches you Touches the apple of His eye.

ZECHARIAH 2:8

When people are mistreating God's inheritance
This action is a serious matter
As if they are assaulting God Himself.
Woe unto these persons!

Comments and Notes:

_____

_____

_____

_____

Day 276

NUGGETS OF TRUTH

So he answered and said to me: This is the word of the Lord to Zerubbabel: Not by might not by power, but by My Spirit, says the Lord of hosts.

ZECHARIAH 4:6

We can't do anything in our own strength.
The Holy Spirit releases the anointing
Enabling us to stand and perform any task.
Lord, I'm nothing without YOU!

Comments and Notes:

Day 277

NUGGETS OF TRUTH

For I am the Lord I do not change; Therefore you are not consumed, O sons of Jacob.

MALACHI 3:6

God is constant and never changes.
HE desires all people to be saved and not destroyed.
God is just and Holy!

Comments and Notes:

Day 278

NUGGETS OF TRUTH

"And all the nations will call you blessed, for you will be a delightful land," says the lord of hosts.

MALACHI 3:12

People will witness the favor
of the Lord on and in your family.
His blessings go before and after you!

Comments and Notes:

_____

_____

_____

_____

_____

Day 279

NUGGETS OF TRUTH

I am the God of Abraham, the God Of Isaac, and the God of Jacob God is not the God of the dead But of the living.

MATTHEW 22:32

**The Blessing of Abraham is of faith;
Also, we serve a true and living God!
Is God alive or dead in your life?**

Comments and Notes:

Day 280

NUGGETS OF TRUTH

But he who is greatest among you Shall be your servant.

MATTHEW 23:11

A minister is a servant; The Lord promotes a consistent, dedicated
And devoted servant. Do you desire to become great?
Then serve with a cheerful heart without getting paid!

Comments and Notes:

_____

_____

_____

_____

_____

_____

Day 281

NUGGETS OF TRUTH

And whoever exalts himself will be Humbled, and he who humbles himself will be exalted.

MATTHEW 23:12

A person that promotes himself
Shall be lower in rank;
Also he that lowers himself will be shown honor.

Comments and Notes:

Day 282

NUGGETS OF TRUTH

But of that day and hour no one knows, not even the angels of heaven, but My Father only.

MATTHEW 24:36

Even the angels in heaven are unaware
Of the coming of the Lord.
God is the only one with this knowledge.
Don't be deceived by false prophets!

Comments and Notes:

Day 283

NUGGETS OF TRUTH

But as the days of Noah were, so also will the coming of the Son of Man be.

MATTHEW 24:37

People will be engaging in every day events
When the Lord returns.
Will you be alert or cradled to sleep?

Comments and Notes:

Day 284

NUGGETS OF TRUTH

For as in the days before the flood, They were eating and drinking, Marrying and giving in marriage, Until the day that Noah entered the ark.

MATTHEW 24:38

Some people will be caught off guard,
When the end comes.
They will be engaged in normal affairs in life.
There's nothing wrong with these things.
But one should be rapture ready at all times!

Comments and Notes:

_____

_____

_____

Day 285

NUGGETS OF TRUTH

Therefore be ready, for the Son of Man is coming at an hour you do not expect.

MATTHEW 24:44

It is urgent that a person
Is alert and ready to meet JESUS!
He will come back unexpectedly.
Will you pray this prayer?
COME LORD JESUS!

Comments and Notes:

_____

_____

_____

_____

_____

Day 286

NUGGETS OF TRUTH

And Jesus came and spoke to them saying, "All authority has be given to Me in Heaven and on earth."

MATTHEW 28:18

Our Lord is Supreme in power
Over the heavens and the earth.
He has absolute authority!

Comments and Notes:

Day 287

NUGGETS OF TRUTH

Go therefore and make disciples Of all the nations, baptizing them in the name of the Father and of the Son and of the Holy Spirit.

MATTHEW 28:19

This is the great commission given to
All believers to disciple people
On the entire surface on the earth.
How many persons have you led to Jesus?
Selah!

Comments and Notes:

_____

_____

_____

_____

Day 288

NUGGETS OF TRUTH

Teaching them to observe all things That I have commanded you; and lo I am with you always, even to the end of the age.
Amen

MATTHEW 28:20

**People have to be taught the requirements
For living a Holy obedient lifestyle.
Before teaching others lead by example!**

Comments and Notes:

_____

_____

_____

_____

Day 289

NUGGETS OF TRUTH

The time is fulfilled, and
The kingdom of God is at hand.
Repent, and believe in the gospel.

MARK 1:15

Repentance is the first step
In being forgiven, then becoming
Born-again because Jesus is coming soon!
Are you ready?

Comments and Notes:

_____

_____

_____

_____

_____

Day 290

NUGGETS OF TRUTH

Then Jesus said to them, "Follow Me And I will make you become fishers Of men."

MARK 1:17

Following Jesus means learning
To seek out men or women
To become disciples!
The spiritual fishing ponds are overflowing.
The Word of the Lord is the bait!

Comments and Notes:

_____

_____

_____

_____

_____

Day 291

NUGGETS OF TRUTH

*But He said to them,
"Let us go into the
Next towns, that I may
preach there also,
Because for this purpose
I have come forth."*

MARK 1:38

There are divine opportunities to minister
The word of the Lord;
Some from the North, South,
East and West. Jesus came into
The Ministry for this cause.
Do you know what your gift is?

Comments and Notes:

Day 292

NUGGETS OF TRUTH

Listen! Behold a sower went out to Sow.

MARK 4:3

One must be willing to obey the voice
Of the Lord when he nudges you,
To release seed on fertile moist soil for
Supernatural growth and increase!
What seed have you sown lately?

Comments and Notes:

_____

_____

_____

_____

_____

Day 293

And it happen, as he sowed, that Some seed fell by the wayside; And the birds of the air came And devoured it.

MARK 4:4

Be careful that your seed
Falls on good ground.
Then watch for the fowls of the air
They are searching for food at all times!

Comments and Notes:

Day 294

Nuggets of Truth

Some fell on stony ground, where it did not have much earth; and immediately it sprang up because it had no depth of earth.

Mark 4:5

Seed that falls on rock that resembles stone
Will not grow because there's
No dirt for cultivation.
How deep is your soil?

Comments and Notes:

_____

_____

_____

_____

_____

Day 295

NUGGETS OF TRUTH

But other seed fell on good ground
And yield a crop that sprang up,
Increased and produced:
Some thirtyfold,
Some sixty and some a hundred.

MARK 4:8

In the correct moisture of fertile rich soil
There will be a great continuous and
Bountiful harvest!

Comments and Notes:

_____

_____

_____

_____

Day 296

NUGGETS OF TRUTH

*Now a certain woman had a flow
Of blood for twelve years,
And had suffered many things from
Many physicians. She had spent
All that she had and was no better,
But rather grew worse.*

MARK 5:25-26

This woman was wealthy at one time.
She had a blood disorder for twelve years.
Her doctor bills increased over time.
She was broke without medical insurance.
Where do you turn when there's no income?

Comments and Notes:

_____

_____

Day 297

Nuggets of Truth

For she said, "If only I may touch His clothes, I shall be made well."

Mark 5:28

This woman made up her mind
That if she could touch the clothes of Jesus,
she would be healed.
As we declare and decree God's
Word we receive the desired results.

Comments and Notes:

Day 298

Nuggets of Truth

Immediately the fountain of her blood was dried up, and she felt in her body that She was healed of the affliction.

Mark 5:29

One touch from the Lord
Stopped her blood disease immediately.
She was ill for twelve years.
How long will you put up with your disorder?

Comments and Notes:

_____

_____

_____

_____

_____

Day 299

NUGGETS OF TRUTH

And Jesus, immediately knowing in Himself that the power had gone out of Him, turned around in the crowd and said, "Who touched my clothes?"

MARK 5:30

The power of God was released
From His body because her faith
Connected with His.
When was the last time you experienced
The tangible power of God?

Comments and Notes:

_____

_____

_____

Day 300

NUGGETS OF TRUTH

But the woman, fearing and trembling knowing what had happen to her, came and fell down before Him and told Him The whole truth.

MARK 5:33

Even though this woman was afraid
Because of her unclean state of being, her life was on the line.
She confessed to Jesus the entire truth,
Then fell down and worshipped Him.
Do you bow in the presence of the Lord?

Comments and Notes:

Day 301

NUGGETS OF TRUTH

And He said to her, "Daughter, your Faith has made you well. Go in peace, and be healed of your affliction."

MARK 5:34

Jesus called her His daughter,
Because she was saved by Faith,
Then healing was the result.
Healing belongs to the children of God!

Comments and Notes:

Day 302

NUGGETS OF TRUTH

And you shall love the Lord your God with all your (mind and) heart and with all your entire being and with all your might.

DEUTERONOMY 6:5 - AMP

A person must love the Lord with their entire being. This includes: mind, will, emotion, body, soul Spirit! Is your love limited to the natural man only?

Comments and Notes:

_____

_____

_____

_____

_____

Day 303

NUGGETS OF TRUTH

*He has shown you, O man, what
Is good. And what does the Lord
require of you
But to do justly, and to love
Kindness and mercy, and to humble
Yourself and walk humbly
With your God?*

MICAH 6:8 - AMP

The Lord has revealed His plans for us
It includes: to do justice, love kindness,
Show mercy and to walk in humility with God!
Before honor humility is exhibited!

Comments and Notes:

Day 304

Nuggets of Truth

By this shall all (men) know that you Are my disciples, if you love one Another (if you keep on showing Love among yourselves.)

John 13:35 - AMP

A true mark of discipleship is LOVE.
This example is a witness to all men.
Are you known to men by a spirit of pride or love?

Comments and Notes:

_____

_____

_____

_____

_____

Day 305

NUGGETS OF TRUTH

And know abideth faith, hope, Charity, these three, but the greatest of these is charity (love).

1 CORINTHIANS 13:13

Love is the greatest gift.
Faith, hope and charity respond to Love!
Are there any gifts operating in your life?

Comments and Notes:

Day 306

NUGGETS OF TRUTH

I am distressed for you,
My brother Jonathan;
very pleasant have
You been to me.
Your love to me was wonderful,
passing the love of women.

2 SAMUEL 1:26 - AMP

When Agape love exists between brothers
This kind of love surpasses love
Between a man or woman.
Agape is Spiritual the kind Jesus has for
His covenant children!

Comments and Notes:

Day 307

NUGGETS OF TRUTH

No one has greater love (No one has shown stronger affection) than to lay down (give up) his own life for his friends.

JOHN 15:13 - AMP

A genuine friend strongest asset
Is to give his/her life for someone else.
Our Elder Brother Jesus did this for mankind!

Comments and Notes:

Day 308

NUGGETS OF TRUTH

O love the Lord, all you His saints! The Lord preserves the faithful, and plentifully pays back him who deals haughtily.

PSALM 31:23 - AMP

The Lord will protect and preserve his Holy people
But the proud or arrogant one
Who does evil will receive a payment!
Will you receive grace or judgment?

Comments and Notes:

_____

_____

_____

_____

Day 309

NUGGETS OF TRUTH

Whereas the object and purpose Of our instructions and charge Is love, which springs from a pure heart and a good (clear) conscience and sincere (unfeigned) faith.

1 TIMOTHY 1:5 - AMP

We have been given instructions for showing love.
So, this is our objective and purpose
Which comes from a sincere heart.
What's in your heart?

Comments and Notes:

_____

_____

_____

Day 310

NUGGETS OF TRUTH

There is no fear in love, but full
grown love turns fear out
Of doors and expels every trace
Of terror! For fear brings with it
The thought of punishment, and
So he who is afraid has not
Reached the full maturity of love
Is not yet grown into
Loves complete perfection.

1 JOHN 4:18 - AMP

Love doesn't dread, it's complete,
Mature, expels every trace of fear.
If one is afraid to love then you have not
Reached full maturity.

Comments and Notes:

Day 311

Nuggets of Truth

If you really love Me, You will keep (obey) My commands.

JOHN 14:15 - AMP

**OBEDIENCE IS THE KEY
TO LOVING GOD!
Are you a doer of the word of God?**

Comments and Notes:

Day 312

NUGGETS OF TRUTH

Such hope never disappoints Or deludes or shames us, for God's Love has been poured out in our hearts through the Holy Spirit Who has been given to us.

ROMANS 5:5 - AMP

Love doesn't lead a person from the truth
Nor disappoints true love is released
In our hearts through the Holy Spirit!

Comments and Notes:

_____

_____

_____

_____

Day 313

NUGGETS OF TRUTH

*Love endures long
and is patient and kind;
Lover never is envious
nor boils over with
Jealousy, is not boastful
or vainglorious,
Does not display itself haughtily.*

1 CORINTHIANS 13:4 - AMP

**Love remains long, is not jealous
But patient, gentle and is not easily provoked!**

Comments and Notes:

_____

_____

_____

Day 314

NUGGETS OF TRUTH

*Now Israel loved Joseph more than
All his children because he was the
Son of his old age,
And he made him a (distinctive)
Long tunic with sleeves.*

GENESIS 37:3 - AMP

Israel loved his son Joseph more than
His other sons because he was old when
He was born. So He made him a
Special coat of many colors?
When God anoints us even our clothes are
A designer original!

Comments and Notes:

_____

_____

_____

Day 315

NUGGETS OF TRUTH

Beloved, let us love one another, For love is (springs from God; and he who loves (his fellowmen) is begotten (born of God and is coming (progressively) to know and understand God (to perceive and recognize and get a better and clearer knowledge of Him).

1 JOHN 4:7 - AMP

Love springs forth from God and shows
That we love our brothers.
This is a clear sign that one has a better
And clearer working knowledge of Him!

Comments and Notes:

Day 316

NUGGETS OF TRUTH

And we know (understand, recognize, are conscience of, by observation and by experience) and believe (adhere to and put faith in and rely on) the love of God cherishes for us. God is love, and he who dwells and continues in God, and God dwells and continues in him.

1 JOHN 4:16 - AMP

God is love therefore we know, understand and have confidence in God's love for us!

Comments and Notes:

Day 317

NUGGETS OF TRUTH

For the love of money is a root of all evils; It is through this craving that some have been led astray and have wandered from the faith and pierced themselves through with many acute (mental) pangs.

1 TIMOTHY 6:10 - AMP

There's nothing wrong with having money
As long as it doesn't have you and one
Is not in love with money.
Some Christians have left their faith
And now is seeking out and after worldly desires.
God's favor will surpass money all of the time!

Comments and Notes:

_____

_____

Day 318

NUGGETS OF TRUTH

Get wisdom! Get understanding! Do not forget, nor turn away from the words of my mouth.

PROVERBS 4:5

The words of God's mouth refer to the Bible.
One needs Godly wisdom and understanding
In order to conduct ourselves correctly!
Stop receiving advice from social media. Go to the word!

Comments and Notes:

Day 319

NUGGETS OF TRUTH

The beginning of Wisdom is: Get wisdom (skilled and godly Wisdom)! (For skillful and godly Wisdom is the principal thing.) And with all you have gotten, get understanding discernment, Comprehension, and interpretation).

PROVERBS 4:7 - AMP

Wisdom is the beginning of skillful and Godly wisdom. This is the foundation for understanding, Discernment, comprehension and interpretation!

Comments and Notes:

Day 320

NUGGETS OF TRUTH

Then Job answered, No doubt you are the (only wise) people (in the world), and wisdom will die with you.

JOB 12:1-2 - AMP

**Sometimes a person may feel
Inferior to others
God's wisdom last throughout eternity!**

Comments and Notes:

_____

_____

_____

_____

_____

Day 321

NUGGETS OF TRUTH

And Jesus increased in wisdom (in broad and full understanding) and in stature and years, and in favor with God and man.

LUKE 2:52 - AMP

**Living a Holy lifestyle brings
Favor with God and man;
And godly wisdom and understanding
Is following close behind!**

Comments and Notes:

_____

_____

_____

_____

_____

Day 322

NUGGETS OF TRUTH

In Gibeon the Lord appeared to Solomon in a dream by night. And God said, "Ask what shall I give you?"

1 KINGS 3:5 - AMP

If the Lord visited you in a dream,
And asked what shall He give you?
What would be your answer?

Comments and Notes:

_____

_____

_____

_____

_____

Day 323

NUGGETS OF TRUTH

Now O Lord my God, You have made your servant king instead of David your father, and I am but a lad (in wisdom and experience); I know not how to go Out (begin) or come in (finish).

1 KINGS 3:7 - AMP

Solomon talked with the Lord
Then told Him he was inexperienced;
And asked for God's help!
Does pride keep you from being honest with God?

Comments and Notes:

_____

_____

_____

Day 324

NUGGETS OF TRUTH

So give Your servant an understanding mind a hearing heart to judge Your people, that I may discern Between good and bad. For who is able to judge And rule this great people?

1 KINGS 3:9 - AMP

Solomon asked for wisdom and understanding.
He knew that this would be needed in order
To execute mercy and justice for all.
If you are a leader, do you show partiality?

Comments and Notes:

_____

_____

Day 325

NUGGETS OF TRUTH

It pleased the Lord that Solomon had asked this.

1 KINGS 3:10 - AMP

The Lord admired Solomon's request.
We must avoid selfish prayers.
Is the Lord pleased with your prayers?

Comments and Notes:

Day 326

NUGGETS OF TRUTH

Behold I have done as you asked. I have given you a wise, discerning mind, so that no one before you was your equal, nor shall any rise after you equal to you.

1 KINGS 3:12 - AMP

The Lord answered Solomon's prayers. He anointed and favored him above all current and future kings. The Lord made his name great!

Comments and Notes:

_____

_____

_____

_____

Day 327

NUGGETS OF TRUTH

I have also given you what you have Not asked, both riches and honor, So that there shall any rise after you Equal to you all your days.

1 KINGS 3:13 - AMP

God also gave him riches and honor.
This was something he didn't ask for.
When a person seeks after God
He will add material blessings as well.
Are you chasing after Father God or things?

Comments and Notes:

Day 328

NUGGETS OF TRUTH

*And if you will go My way,
Keep my statutes and my
commandments
As your father David did, then I
Will lengthen your days.*

1 KINGS 3:14 - AMP

It is awesome when the Lord speaks
To us face to face. Likewise, He reminded
Solomon that if he kept his statues like David
Did then his life span would be lengthened.

Comments and Notes:

_____

_____

_____

_____

Day 329

NUGGETS OF TRUTH

If any of you is deficient in wisdom, Let him ask of the giving God (Who gives) to everyone liberally and ungrudgingly, without reproaching or faultfinding, and it will be given him.

JAMES 1:5 - AMP

A person who is lacking in wisdom
Needs to go to the power source.
One must ask the Living giving God
For it; He is not stingy and gives liberally.

Comments and Notes:

_____

_____

_____

Day 330

NUGGETS OF TRUTH

For this world's wisdom is foolishness (absurdity and stupidity) with God, For it is written, He lays hold of the wise in their own craftiness.

1 CORINTHIANS 3:19 - AMP

The wisdom from the world is foolish
And deceitful, only bringing destruction with it;
Compared to Skillful and Godly wisdom from God.
God's wisdom will always cause increase!

Comments and Notes:

_____
_____
_____
_____
_____

Day 331

NUGGETS OF TRUTH

For in much (human) wisdom is Much vexation, and he who increases Knowledge increases sorrow.

ECCLESIASTES 1:18 - AMP

In our own mind there is much instability.
Also, knowledge can cause grief
Because it bring jealousy and strife.
Don't allow the enemy to prevent
You from receiving revelation knowledge
From studying God's word!

Comments and Notes:

_____

_____

_____

_____

_____

Day 332

NUGGETS OF TRUTH

For to the person who pleases Him God gives wisdom and knowledge and joy; but to the sinner He gives the work of gathering and heaping up, that he may give to one who pleases God. This also is vanity and a striving after the wind and a feeding on it.

ECCLESIASTES 2:26 - AMP

As a person pleases God He releases Wisdom and knowledge into their being. The sinner's revenue will be transferred Into a Christian's life.

Comments and Notes:

Day 333

NUGGETS OF TRUTH

Saying in a loud voice, Deserving is the Lamb, who was sacrificed, to receive all the power and riches and wisdom and might and honor and majesty (glory, splendor) And blessing!

REVELATION 5:12

Declare and decree that Jesus is worthy
Of all praise, honor, glory and dominion
Because He is a Blessing to everyone
Who receives Him as Lord and Savior without being ashamed.
Do you know Him as Lord and Savior?

Comments and Notes:

Day 334

Nuggets of Truth

And to the one he gave five talents, To another two, and to another one, To each according to his own ability; And immediately he went on a journey.

Matthew 25:15

Everyone who is born again
Has at least one talent.
Will you multiply your gift
Or prostitute it to the highest bidder?

Comments and Notes:

_____

_____

_____

_____

Day 335

NUGGETS OF TRUTH

Having then gifts differing according
To the grace that is given to us,
Let us use them; if prophecy, let us
Prophesy in proportion to our faith;
Or ministry let us use
It in our ministering;
He who teaches, in teaching.

ROMANS 12:6-7 - AMP

Grace is an anointing that is given by God
In order for your gift to be effective
In the body of Christ.

Comments and Notes:

_____

_____

Day 336

NUGGETS OF TRUTH

Then he who had received the five talents went and traded with them And made another five talents.

MATTHEW 25:16

Serving the Lord by using your talents brings Promotion, growth and increase.
Don't become stagnant by sitting idle in ministry!

Comments and Notes:

_____

_____

_____

_____

_____

Day 337

NUGGETS OF TRUTH

And likewise he who had received two gained two more also.

MATTHEW 25:17

**The Lord will bless your gifts
When one uses them.
Increase is sure to follow.**

Comments and Notes:

Day 338

NUGGETS OF TRUTH

But he who had received one went and dug it the ground, and hid his lord's money.

MATTHEW 25:18

If a person is afraid they will not do anything In order to produce more revenue!

Comments and Notes:

_____

_____

_____

_____

_____

_____

Day 339

NUGGETS OF TRUTH

But his lord answered and said to him, you wicked and lazy servant, you knew that I reap where I have not sown, and gather where I have not scattered seed.

MATTHEW 25:26

Jesus will count a person as being lazy
When one will not plant their seed
To produce more fruit.
Are you yielding a harvest?

Comments and Notes:

_____

_____

_____

_____

Day 340

NUGGETS OF TRUTH

Therefore take the talent from him, and give it to him who has ten talents.

MATTHEW 25:28

Do not allow your gift to be taken away
And given to another because they multiplied their seed.
You have the same opportunity!

Comments and Notes:

Day 341

NUGGETS OF TRUTH

For everyone who has, more will be given, and he will have abundance; but from him who does not have, even what he has will be taken away.

MATTHEW 25:29

A person who has wealth more is given
Because this person sows into other lives.
While a person with a little
Even that is taken away due to
One having a tight fist!
What's in your hands? Do you bless others?

Comments and Notes:

_____

_____

_____

Day 342

NUGGETS OF TRUTH

Bring all the tithes into the storehouse, that there may be food in my house,
And try me in this,
Says the LORD of hosts.

MALACHI 3:10A

Give one-tenth of your gross earnings
To a Bible-based faith Church.
So that God's house is provided for.
Test the Lord and see if He will
Not take care of your household needs!

Comments and Notes:

_____

_____

_____

Day 343

NUGGETS OF TRUTH

If I will not open for you the Windows of heaven And pour out for you such blessing That there will not be room enough to receive it.

MALACHI 3:10b

The windows of heaven has many outlets of God's blessings. There will be a continually flow of abundance.
At this time you will be able to assist others!
Are you the Lord's distribution center yet?

Comments and Notes:

_____

_____

_____

Day 344

NUGGETS OF TRUTH

*I fast twice a week;
I give tithes of all that I possess.*

LUKE 18:12

Fasting and tithing is good, but should be
Done in secret as unto the Lord!
Boasting is done out of our flesh!
Are you a show off? If so you have your reward now!

Comments and Notes:

_____

_____

_____

_____

_____

Day 345

NUGGETS OF TRUTH

Honor the Lord with your possessions, and with the first fruits of all your increase;
So your barns will be filled with Plenty and your vats will Overflow with new wine.

PROVERBS 3:9-10

Acknowledge the Lord as the source and provider
Of all things that you enjoy.
So, His anointing will increase on your
Life and His favor go before you at all times.
Are you experiencing financial growth?

Comments and Notes:

_____

_____

Day 346

NUGGETS OF TRUTH

But Ruth said: "Entreat me not to leave you, or to turn back from following after you; For wherever you go, I will go; and wherever you lodge, I will lodge; your people shall Be my people; And God, my God."

RUTH 1:16

Ruth was willing to give up everything
To be with her mother-in-law.
What will your cost be in assisting someone else?

Comments and Notes:

_____

_____

Day 347

NUGGETS OF TRUTH

Then they lifted up their voices
And wept again, and Oprah kissed
Her mother in law but
Ruth clung to her.

RUTH 1:14

Oprah gave Naomi a good bye kiss
Whereas, Ruth embraced Naomi.

Comments and Notes:
_____
_____
_____
_____
_____
_____

Day 348

NUGGETS OF TRUTH

*Then he said,
Blessed are you of the Lord,
My daughter! For you have shown
More kindness at the end than
At the beginning, in that you
Did not go after young men,
Whether poor or rich.*

RUTH 3:10

Boaz pronounced a blessing over Ruth
Because she stayed with Naomi; and did not
Leave to find a husband!
Will you allow a man to find you as his wife?

Comments and Notes:

_____

_____

Day 349

NUGGETS OF TRUTH

And now my daughter, do not fear. I will do for you all that you request, For all the people of my town know that you are a virtuous woman.

RUTH 3:11

Boaz heard about Ruth's history; then gave her favor because she was an honorable woman. Be mindful regarding your reputation! Are you willing to live a holy life before God and man?

Comments and Notes:

_____

_____

_____

Day 350

NUGGETS OF TRUTH

So Boaz took Ruth and she Became his wife; and when he went In to her, the Lord gave her conception, and she bore a son.

RUTH 4:13

Boaz married Ruth and the Lord
Blessed their union, she became pregnant
And a son was born. It's important to get married
before having children
This is God ordained!

Comments and Notes:

_____

_____

_____

_____

Day 351

NUGGETS OF TRUTH

Watch and pray, lest you enter Into temptation. The spirit indeed Is willing, but the flesh is weak.

MATTHEW 26:41

When one is given the opportunity
To pray before an event stay in the guide lines,
Focused on the assignment!
Interceding for others is an honor!

Comments and Notes:

_____

_____

_____

_____

_____

_____

Day 352

NUGGETS OF TRUTH

*Now it came to pass,
As He was praying in a certain place, when He ceased,
that one of his disciples
Said to Him, "Lord, teach us
How to pray as John also taught his disciples."*

LUKE 11:1

One should be specific regarding praying,
Whoever the leader is may provide instructions.
It is important to follow it closely!
Obedience is important to the Lord!

Comments and Notes:

Day 353

NUGGETS OF TRUTH

Therefore I exhort first of all That supplications, prayers, intercessions and giving of thanks be made for all men. For kings and all who are in authority, that we may lead a quiet and peaceable Life, in all godliness and reverence.

1 TIMOTHY 2: 1-2

It is important to pray for all men;
Next, then those who are in authority.
The reason is so that one may lead
A quiet and peaceable life!

Comments and Notes:

Day 354

NUGGETS OF TRUTH

We know that God does not listen to sinners; But if anyone is God-fearing and a worshiper of Him and does His will, He listens to him.

JOHN 9:31

The LORD doesn't hear sinner's prayers
Except that of repentance.
He acknowledges Christian prayers that
Does His will and listens.

Comments and Notes:

_____

_____

_____

_____

_____

Day 355

NUGGETS OF TRUTH

For the wages which sin pays is death, but the (bountiful) free gift of God Is eternal life through (in union with) Jesus Christ our Lord.

ROMANS 6:23 -AMP

The penalty of sinning is death.
However, there is an ultimate gift from God
That is eternal life through Jesus Christ!

Comments and Notes:

_____

_____

_____

Day 356

NUGGETS OF TRUTH

*And he brought them out
(of the dungeon)
And said,
men what is necessary for me
To do that I may be saved?*

ACTS 16:30 - AMP

After a person has a wilderness experience
God's grace of salvation is always available.
But, it is not wise to wait until one
Is on their death bed!

Comments and Notes:

_____

_____

_____

_____

Day 357

NUGGETS OF TRUTH

For everyone who calls upon the name of the Lord (Invoking Him as Lord) Will be saved.

ROMANS 10:13 - AMP

Salvation is available to everyone
Or anyone that calls on Jesus name by Faith!
Have you called Him Savior yet?

Comments and Notes:

Day 358

NUGGETS OF TRUTH

*But Jesus said to the woman,
Your faith has saved you;
Go (enter) into peace
In freedom from all your distresses
That you are experienced as the
result of sin).*

LUKE 7:50 - AMP

The woman's faith saved her,
Then Jesus released peace in her life.
The Lord desires to do the same thing for us!
God's peace is a benefit of Salvation!

Comments and Notes:

_____

_____

_____

Day 359

NUGGETS OF TRUTH

But I obtained mercy for the reason that in me, as the foremost (of sinners), Jesus Christ might show forth and display all His perfect Long-suffering and patience for an example to those who would thereafter believe on Him for (the gaining of) eternal life.

1 TIMOTHY 1:16 - AMP

Paul received mercy from the Lord. He labeled himself as a chief sinner. The lord extended these graces, His patience, loving kindness is extended to all. However, one must repent and receive Jesus as Lord of their life.

Comments and Notes:

Day 360

NUGGETS OF TRUTH

For such (praying) is good and right, and (it is pleasing and acceptable to God our Savior, who wishes all men to be saved and (increasingly) to perceive and recognize and discern and know precisely and correctly the (divine) Truth.

1 TIMOTHY 2:3-4 - AMP

One must pray the prayer of faith
In order to receive Salvation;
Our Lord doesn't want any to perish
But have eternal life.

Comments and Notes:

Day 361

Nuggets of Truth

For it is by free grace (God's unmerited favor) that you are saved (delivered from judgment and made partakers of Christ's salvation) Through (your) faith. And this (salvation) is not of yourselves (Of your own doing, it came not through your own striving), But it is the gift of God

Ephesians 2:8 - Amp

A person has the ability to receive God's grace.
This grace is not earned, it's a gift
Not by any works, but from our creator.
Will you receive Him today?

Comments and Notes:

Day 362

NUGGETS OF TRUTH

You must also be ready therefore, For the Son of Man is coming at an hour when you do not expect Him.

MATTHEW 24:44 - AMP

**Are you preparing for Jesus Christ return? It is imperative to live
A holy lifestyle every day,
Because He is coming without
An announcement! Selah**

Comments and Notes:

Day 363

NUGGETS OF TRUTH

Therefore He is able also to save To the uttermost (completely, perfectly, finally, and for all time and eternity) those who come to God through Him, since He is always living to make petition to God and intercede with Him and intervene for them.

HEBREWS 7:25 - AMP

Jesus has sufficient ability to redeem, Rescue and make free anyone that desires salvation. He is constantly praying to the father on our behalf! Selah!

Comments and Notes:

Day 364

NUGGETS OF TRUTH

For God is not unrighteous to forget or overlook your labor and the love which you have shown for His names sake in the ministering to the needs of the saints (His own consecrated people) as you still do.

HEBREWS 6:10 - AMP

Because Abba Father's nature is Holy and righteous, He is constantly aware of our stewardship and vocation that
One gifts for kingdom building. He is mindful that this is done for His glory and people; that are consecrated, set apart for
His purpose. You will receive a harvest from Him! Selah!

Comments and Notes:

Day 365

NUGGETS OF TRUTH

Besides this you know what (a critical) hour this is, how it is high time now for you to wake up out of your sleep (rouse to reality). For salvation (final deliverance) is nearer to us now than when we first believed.

ROMANS 13:11 - AMP

You must know and perceive this one thing; it is crucial that one remain steadfast in Holy living and being a doer of God's word. The Lord's return is nearer than ever. Do not become a sluggard in your Christian walk or dedication to God. One's very life and legacy depends on this.
Selah!

Comments and Notes:

About the Author

Sara Haywood is the founder, Elder and CEO of Anointed Vessels Ministries of Ozark, Al. The ministry is founded on the Word of God. The mission is to disciple all men (women) to the point of change by salvation. The ministry was founded in 2008, focused on widows at the time. Since then the ministry is opened to all people.

Sara is married to Willie, they have four children; one son-in-law (Carlos/Shanell Bailey, Lamonzo, Naomi, Reggie) and two grandchildren (Lamar and Nivea Sa'ri).

Sara has published "Abundant Living Encouragement for Success", is now a conference speaker; and has newly founded a "Community Outreach Event" established in 2015.

The objective is to reach people in the surrounding areas to help supplement physical needs, while providing spiritual guidance. This is a no cost event or obligation!

Sara is an active member of Acts Church Christian Center Inc. Dothan, Al; Pastor Jack Beachem Jr. and minister Lamesha are the shepherds. She serves as elder, evangelist, minister, intercessor and teacher. Sara enjoys sharing the love of Christ with others and encouraging them with her victories that she has won through Jesus Christ. Remember, God is Faithful to those who are faithful to Him! Thank you, Holy Father!

" It is written: Man shall not live by bread alone, but by every word that proceeds from the mouth of the Lord." (Matthew 4:4) "Everything begins with the word!"

Your feedback and comments are welcome.
Anointed Vessels Ministries
Elder Sara Haywood
P.O. Box 783 Ozark, Al 36361
sarahaywood835@yahoo.com

www.ingramcontent.com/pod-product-compliance
Lightning Source LLC
Chambersburg PA
CBHW071647090426
42738CB00009B/1446